Steel Chariots in the Desert

Steel Chariots in the Desert

The First World War Experiences of a Rolls Royce
Armoured Car Driver with the Duke of
Westminster in Libya and in Arabia
with T.E. Lawrence

S. C. Rolls

LEONAUR

Steel Chariots in the Desert: The First World War Experiences of a Rolls Royce Armoured Car Driver with the Duke of Westminster in Libya and in Arabia with T. E. Lawrence

Originally published in 1937 under the
title *Steel Chariots in the Desert*

Published by Leonaur Ltd

Material original to this edition and its origination in
this form copyright © 2005 Leonaur Ltd

ISBN (10 digit): 1-84677-019-X (hardcover)
ISBN (13 digit): 978-1-84677-019-7 (hardcover)

ISBN (10 digit) 1-84677-005-X (softcover)
ISBN (13 digit): 978-1-84677-005-0 (softcover)

http://www.leonaur.com

Publishers Notes

In the interests of authenticity, the spellings, grammar and place names used
in this book have been retained from the original edition.

The opinions of the author represent a view of events in which he was a
participant related from his own perspective;
as such the text is relevant as an historical document.

The views expressed in this book are not necessarily
those of the publisher.

Contents

List of Illustrations.

Preface

Ever since the armistice of 1918 I had had a desire to amplify my rough war diary into a full narrative; but it was not until the autumn of 1935 that I felt a sufficient urge to enable me to complete the work in the spare time left to me by my profession. The final incentive was given to me by a friendly passage in the foreword to T. E. Lawrence's book Seven Pillars of Wisdom:

And there were many other leaders or lonely fighters to whom this self-regardant picture is not fair. It is still less fair, of course, like all war-stories, to the unnamed rank and file, who miss their share of the credit, as they must do, until they can write the dispatches.

To have written, from memory and a few meagre notes, a strictly accurate description of events which occurred so long ago, even as I understood them at the time, would not have been an easy matter; but this work has been planned ever since its incidents were enacted, and its contents have thus been more firmly held in mind than would otherwise have been the case.

S.C.R.

Chapter One
The Armoured Car Squadron

August 1914! The feverish days rush by with a rapidity that is alarming. The war will be over before one can get within fair hail of honour and glory, before one may taste the rousing draught of adventure. All the old pursuits, ambitions, plans of life, have become blurred and unreal, like memories of daffodils in rose-laden June. There will be enough and to spare of all that when the season comes round again.

Old interests and pursuits have, indeed, lost their hold, and seem almost to have become discredited. Accordingly I, who was employed in the motor industry in which I had served my apprenticeship, and who knew a good deal about motor cars and very little about horses, lost no time in joining the throng of those who were clamouring to join the Northamptonshire Yeomanry. My services were declined.

Back again in Coventry, I turned once more in some dejection to motor cars. At that time there was no motor unit in the fighting forces, except the naval armoured car section which had been formed for service with the Antwerp expedition. But in November I heard that this was being reorganized as an armoured car brigade of the Royal Naval Air Service, and scenting here my opportunity, I again presented myself for enlistment. On my twenty-first birthday, 19th November 1914, I joined at Wormwood Scrubbs, as a petty officer, No. 2 Squadron of this Brigade, of which squadron Major the Duke of Westminster was in command. 'Bull dog', 'Biter', 'Bloodhound', and the others of our twelve Rolls-Royce fighting machines shone with new paint, and seemed to exude gentle hints of savage ferocity.

We remained only a short time in the mud of Wormwood Scrubbs, and were in France on the eve of Neuve Chapelle. Being of little or no use in trench warfare, however, we undertook taxi duty, establishing our depot at the White Chateau on the Poperinghe road. This was the most advanced point considered to be safe for staff cars carrying brass-hatted messengers to the forward areas. At the White Chateau they transferred from their staff cars to our armoured cars, and were taken on to their destination, as far as possible. I have not yet forgotten those mad drives through Ypres, over a road in the actual process of being ploughed up by shells, with my lookout man lying on the front wing shouting, 'Left!' 'Right!' 'Left!' while I peered through the narrow slit in the armour plating at him, and at the fog of smoke and dust which obscured the shattered ground. There were engineers lurking in the skirts of that fog, who tried to fill in the holes as fast as they were torn out, with stones and mud. As we went up through the battered town, past the pulverized ruins of the Cloth Hall, the awful din of bursting shells made the whole place clang again: and so, on through the Menin Gate to the borders of no-man's-land. I stop the car. Out jumps my 'fare', scurries for the nearest trench, and dives into it, thankful, no doubt, to be there with a whole skin. Now to get back through Ypres, and home to the comparative peace of the White Chateau cab rank.

After the first gas attack, when our depot had to be abandoned, and we moved further back, our commanding officer advised us to transfer from the navy to the army, so that we might remain together in a new Brigade which was to be formed. In order to do this we had to return to England, a fact which shows that red tape has its important uses, and after wandering along the French coast from town to town, repudiated by all, for some considerable time, we at last reached London, where we changed from blue clothes into khaki.

We returned to France, but not for long; for on Christmas Eve, 1915, we entrained at St. Omer for Marseilles, and at this port took ship, with our cars, for Alexandria. We were now to test our mettle in the Libyan Desert, in action against the Senussi Arabs.

Chapter Two
The Senussi

The Senussi were a religious brotherhood of Mohammedans whose members were to be found in nearly every Mohammedan country, and especially in the oases and deserts of North Africa and Western Arabia. The brotherhood was founded about a century ago by Mohammed Es Senussi, an Arab of Algeria, descended from the Prophet's daughter Fatima. This man was a puritan reformer, who travelled and preached all over the Libyan desert. He founded monasteries at Mecca and in many towns of North Africa; and among these was the White Monastery, near Derna on the coast of Tripoli. About eighty years ago the Senusite chief settled in the Libyan oasis of Jaghbub, and there his descendants usually maintained their headquarters.

The Senusites extended their influence peacefully all over the desert, from Benghazi to Lake Chad, and from the western border of Egypt far into the Sahara. In those regions the authority of their chief equalled that of a ruling prince. It was an authority used for improving the religious practice of the Arabs and Berbers, for keeping order in the desert, and for encouraging trade. When the Mahdi rose to power in the southern Sudan he invited the Senusites to join him, but they refused to do so; and, until seduced by German gold and Turkish flattery in 1915, they were always friendly to Egypt and its Turkish or English rulers.

They were not friendly, however, to the French, who were continually pushing further into their sphere of influence from the west, nor to the Italians, who wanted to encroach from the coast of Tripoli. The Senusites sided with the Turks in the Italo-Turkish war, and after the defeat of Turkey they continued to fight against the Italian army of occupation. After 1911 Ahmed Es Senussi, the reigning chief, regarded the Italians as his most dangerous foes, and he managed to keep them confined to a narrow strip of territory on the coast.

Early in 1915 Nuri Bey, a half-brother of Enver Pasha, who had landed in Tripoli and made his way to the Senussi headquarters, was trying to induce Ahmed Es Senussi, by means of bribes and the promise of extended power, to throw in his lot with Turkey, declare a holy war and attack Egypt. Ahmed, being friendly to Egypt and to the British there, refused the offer. But in May Italy joined the Allies; and it seems very probable that Ahmed could have kept out of the European war now only by discontinuing his opposition to the Italian invaders, for by some means or other Italy would have dragged her North African affairs into the general scrimmage, and obtained the help of the army in Egypt if he continued to oppose them. With this argument Nuri at last secured the active allegiance of the Senusites to Turkey and the Central Powers. In fact, it was our campaign in the western desert which eventually made Cyrenaica safe for the wilful tricks of infant Fascism.

The Turks now planned a threefold attack on Egypt. Jaafar Pasha - a Baghdad Arab, and general in the Turkish service - who had landed with Nuri from a German submarine, was to lead a force along the coast against Alexandria; Ahmed Es Senussi himself was to advance on Cairo with a large body of his Arabs, from Jaghbub and the Siwa Oasis; and the Sultan of Darfur was to lead a third force against Khartoum. Nuri, who was the prime mover in the whole scheme, was usually present with Jaafar's force.

In the middle of November 1915 the Egyptian coastguard force at Sollum - on the frontier, about 350 miles by road from

Alexandria - had to be withdrawn to Mersa Matruh, in face of the threatening attitude of the Senussi. A week earlier a German submarine had torpedoed the gunboat Tara and also a transport, the Moorina, and had landed the survivors of their crews and passengers at Bardia, north of Sollum, handing them over to the Senusites. This incident, and several attacks made on coastguard garrisons at about the same time, were the causes which finally made General Maxwell, the Commander-in-Chief in Egypt, take action; for Ahmed Es Senussi, though still professing to be friendly, refused to surrender the prisoners.

On Christmas Day a mixed force of New Zealanders, English yeomanry, Indian cavalry and Egyptians succeeded in beating back the advance of Jaafar's force on Matruh, but no real counter-attack could be made until more troops were available. Our armoured cars, which had now been formed into a brigade of three batteries, each consisting of four cars, were a part of the awaited reinforcements.

These war-chariots consisted of 40-50 h.p. Rolls-Royce Alpine chassis, fitted with four-speed gearing, and with a specially strengthened back axle. On this there was mounted a steel cylinder, five feet in diameter, fitted with a revolving turret, and this formed the principal part of the body. Behind it there was an open platform made of wood. The cylinder, the bonnet, the doors covering the front of the radiator, and other details were of specially toughened bullet-proof armour plate, three-eighths of an inch thick. In the turret, which formed the roof of the cylinder, a Vickers-Maxim gun was mounted, its breech end extending a foot into the interior. The heat in the Libyan desert in summer was found to be so great that men inside the cars were in danger of being cooked like rabbits in a saucepan, and in consequence the turrets were removed when we were on reconnaissance work. The Maxim gun was then fixed in a special mounting which allowed it to be turned in any direction, as in the turret. The two armour-plate doors in front of the radiator could be opened or closed by the driver at will. The dash-plate consisted of an armour-plate lid with narrow horizontal slits in it, which enabled the driver to see to some extent when in action. At other times the lid was propped open. In the wall of the cylinder, at the rear, there was a doorway, with double doors of armour, giving on to the platform at the back of the car; and high up in the cylinder at various points there were small apertures, with movable covering plates, through which a rifle could be used.

Each car carried two thin flock mattresses, which, when unrolled in the bottom of the vehicle, just covered the floor. This formed a rather cramped but not uncomfortable bed for two men. Besides these mattresses, the inside equipment consisted of two service rifles, fixed in handy positions, one rubber water-bottle (always religiously kept full) for refilling the water jacket of the Maxim, and a first-aid chest. Ammunition for the gun was stored, loaded ready in belts, in boxes on the rear platform; and there also were two long boxes for carrying a supply of rifles if the necessity should arise. These last, fixed along the sides, served as seats when there were additional passengers.

We had great difficulty in obtaining suitable wheels for the cars. At first we tried filling the tyres with rubber solution, but this was soon given up, as the moment a tyre was damaged by bullets or sharp stones the rubber solution escaped. We also used both single and double wheels at different times, but the latter were soon found to be the more serviceable, not only because a puncture could be disregarded until a normal halt was called, but for other reasons which will appear in the course of my narrative.

The full crew of a car consisted of a driver and two gunners, but as the confined space made it almost impossible for three men to be usefully employed at one time, only two men were carried usually in each vehicle. The driver acted as assistant gunner, making shift as best he could to feed the cartridge-belt into the gun breech with one hand, while managing the steering wheel with the other. Only short men could stand upright in the cylinder; and tall men, who had to half double themselves up, took up very much more room and were always cramped and uncomfortable, and on this account were generally considered the least desirable to work with. Even small men had to crouch when firing the Maxim or a rifle. Most of our fellows were short, and the great height of the Duke of Westminster no doubt added a trial to his pains and fatigues, such as the rest of us were spared.

When on the march driver and gunner sat side by side on the floor, with their legs straight out in front, and their backs supported by two adjustable slings attached by spring hooks to the dash-frame. The motion of the car thus made their bodies swing from side to side. A tall driver sat right down on the floor, but a short one, and most of ours were short, had to make a pile of small square mats to sit on, sufficiently high to give him proper vision through the slits in the front armour. When he had to reverse his engine and drive backwards, the driver unhooked his sling and lay back on one elbow, so as to look through a small aperture in the rear armour door. One of the tests imposed on recruits by the Royal Naval Air Service was driving in reverse in this position at forty miles an hour. Steering was managed with the right hand only, the right foot was moved to the clutch pedal and the hand-throttle used.

When we arrived at Alexandria from Marseilles there was still great danger that Mersa Matruh, with its coastguard fort and wireless station, might fall into the hands of the Senusites at any moment. The place was kept more or less isolated, as far as land communication was concerned, by roving bands of the enemy; and it was considered unlikely that we could reach it by the land route, with our armoured cars intact and ready to support the garrison. It was therefore decided that we should go by sea.

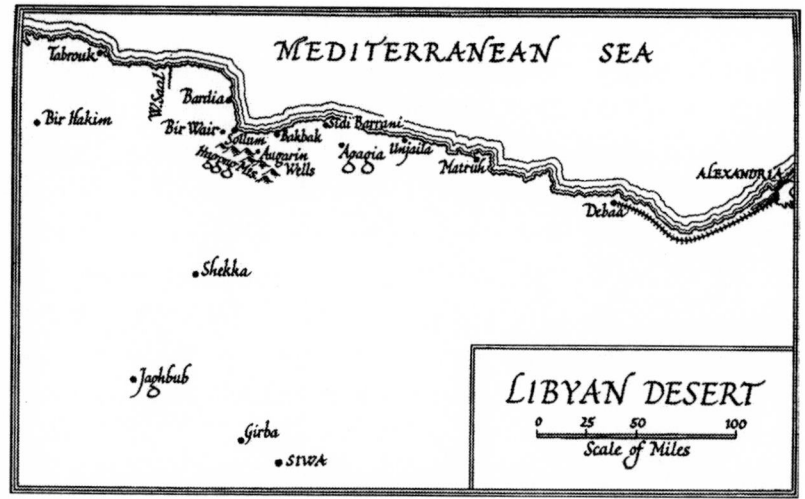

The Libyan Desert.

We embarked in a commandeered Greek steamer, the Borulas, and put to sea, expecting to make Mersa Matruh in fourteen hours. At nightfall, however, a terrific storm leapt out of the east, beating up the sea into huge waves, and throwing the Borulas about like a nutshell. Orders were given to lash the cars in the hold together with ropes, but this was found to be of no use at all, for the ropes snapped like thread, and the heavy cars crashed together, first this way, then that, as the ship lurched and rolled amongst the raging seas. Nearly every man, including the captain and his crew, lay at full length, some on deck and some below, gripping a fixed object. For three nights and two days we saw nothing but agitated water, and tasted neither food nor drink. The only man I remember to have seen in an upright position after the first few hours was the Duke of Westminster, who made his appearance on deck within the limited range of my observation on the second day. The third terrible night wore away at last, and the light of dawn crept over a sea which, with curious suddenness, had become as smooth as glass. Ahead we could see a rocky coast, with the white speck of a fort on one of the heights. This was Mersa

Matruh. Presently a palm fringed lagoon came in sight, and then the minaret and dome of a mosque.

In the tiny harbour the cars were lowered with difficulty into two lighters, which ferried them to the beach; and from there, with the help of occasional pushing by the crews, they were driven through the sand to some stone blockhouses a mile away.

The village had been fortified with rows of trenches, dugouts, gunpits and observation posts, and it looked capable of resisting any attack that Arabs might undertake. We spent a day or two in recovering from the voyage, and then preparations were made for sending out patrols with the object of locating the Senusites. In the first expedition two armoured cars and two Ford tenders accompanied some mounted scouts to the southward, crossed a low range of hills, and came into a perfectly flat and barren desert. We saw nothing else but a solitary hut, and having fired a few rounds at this with our machine guns, we returned. Another day, with four cars, we explored the coast road to westward, but after about thirty miles the road was found to be so bad that the Duke gave orders to return. On one occasion an armoured car broke its rear axle, and, the gun and ammunition having been removed, it was abandoned in the desert for the night, a new axle being taken out to it the next day.

At last we encountered enemy outposts at Unjaila, fifty miles along the coast, a place which General Peyton, commander of our force, had decided to reoccupy. We managed to shoot one of them, and duly reported their presence on our return to Matruh. On 13th February a large force of camel corps and cavalry was sent out to Unjaila, and with them went two armoured cars. I remained at the base and busied myself with making adjustments in my engine with the object of reducing its tendency to overheat in the heavy ground. The next morning stragglers began to come into Matruh, and this continued all day. At three o'clock in the afternoon two car-drivers walked in footsore, in a state of exhaustion. We gathered from their reports that the Senussi had made a feint of retiring, and had drawn our men into an ambush. There had been heavy fighting and many casualties. Before nightfall we moved out, expecting to cover their retirement, and to lend a hand in burying the dead. We buried some bodies, but fortunately found that Colonel Fulton's force had duly occupied Unjaila.

Returning to Matruh, we continued our work of patrolling the desert on all sides of that base until 20th February, when large bodies of troops and long caravans of supplies marched out towards the west for the reoccupation of Sollum, which had been planned by General Peyton. The first move was to be from Unjaila to Sidi Barrani, forty miles further along the coast.

Two days later, after a farewell supper of little eggs, sour bread, and weak coffee, served in the blockhouse restaurant of a bold Greek, who had valiantly followed the army with a supply of these luxuries, and a capacious purse, the Armoured Car Brigade moved out in full strength to Unjaila, followed by wireless and Red Cross cars and other transport. We had gone about forty miles when an aeroplane flew towards us and dropped a message to the effect that Jaafar Pasha with 1500 men, covered by scouts, was stationed at Agagia, to the south of Sidi Barrani. The night was spent at Unjaila, and the next day we accompanied the yeomanry and South African infantry on their march along the coast towards Sidi Barrani. Expecting to be attacked by the enemy at any moment, we drove tensely, the machine gunners with their fingers on their triggers, and the armour lids nearly closed.

At dusk we descended into a slight hollow, and there camped for the night, the armoured cars being drawn up in a circle round the transport, with guns pointing out. The empty desert about us was as silent as the grave, and we had seen no sign of the enemy. With her armoured doors open, my car, 'Blast' by name, offered a not uncomfortable bed, and with my head resting under the dashboard, near the clutch pedal, and my feet hanging out of the doorway, I slept soundly in spite of the heat and mosquitoes.

With the first sign of dawn those who had slept on the sand threw off their dew-soaked blankets, and the camp began to bustle in the cold desert air. Breakfast consisted of bully beef, biscuits and tea, and within an hour the armoured cars and cavalry were again moving towards the west, followed by the infantry and transport. The desert was occasionally broken by small watercourses, and after advancing cautiously for some miles we came upon a deserted camping-place of the enemy's main body in the Wadi Mehtila, and there a halt was ordered. The following day, while our scouts were busied in examining the enemy's position, seven miles inland, the remainder of the force rested in camp. In the afternoon there was some shelling by both sides, but no attack.

Before dawn on 26th February the cavalry rode out to reconnoitre, and soon the whole force, except the transport and a small guard, was on the move to the southward. Presently an order came that two of the cars, 'Blast' and 'Bulldog,' were to cover the right flank of the Dorset Yeomanry in their coming attempt to get behind the enemy's position. We drove the cars to a hill on which our headquarters were established, and there I took up a staff officer, while 'Bulldog' accommodated a gunner. The cavalry was massed in concealment behind the hill.

Two thousand yards away there were a number of sand dunes, on the slopes of which the Senussi were entrenched. The infantry were to make a frontal attack on the position, with the yeomanry guarding their right flank and working round to the enemy's rear.

While the infantry were advancing the Dorset Yeomanry dismounted and went in on foot. When they had gone some distance we raced away from our hill in fine style, but unfortunately both cars soon became bogged in the loose sand on the plain. We had managed to get within easy machine-gun range of the enemy, however, and, whipping the guns from their mountings, the gunners ran with them to the nearest high point, followed by the drivers with the tripods. The yeomanry, deployed on the plain, were still advancing towards the enemy position, and bullets were flying all about us. We could plainly see the Arabs moving here and there in their entrenchments, and we swept their position with belt after belt from our machine guns.

The infantry attack lasted for some hours, but at last we ceased our fire as they overran the Senussi front line. The enemy melted away amongst the sand-hills, and the horses of the Dorset Yeomanry were moved up closer, so that they could mount. Then the cavalry rode away southward, so as to get behind the Senussi. Looking through my glasses I could presently see a great mob of the Arabs streaming out of the hills, and retreating further into the desert; and not long afterwards I saw that the Dorset Yeomanry were galloping after them. Some of the men and horses fell, but the rest quickly closed with the running enemy, and scattered them with their swords. This fine charge brought the action to an end, nothing being left to be done except to pursue the fugitives. This had to be left to the yeomanry, as we could not move our cars. I particularly noticed a Turk galloping towards the horizon on a beautiful piebald horse. It was Nuri Bey, the chief plotter of the Senussi rising. He and I were to meet later as comrades. Jaafar was captured by the yeomanry.

After the fight we returned to our base in the Wadi Mehtila, and two days later we followed the South African infantry into Sidi Barrani, where no opposition was met with. This stronghold, eighty-five miles west of Matruh, had been in the hands of the enemy for three months past. From here I returned to Matruh in a tender, to help in bringing the other Armoured Car Batteries from that place to Sidi Barrani.

Although called the Khedival Road, the track between the two places was not a metalled highway. It had been made by throwing aside the larger stones on the desert, or dumping them on the patches of soft sand. As we came in sight of the fort of Sidi Barrani again, after our drive of eighty-five miles over a desert broken only by occasional ruins of tombs and hovels, by bleached bones of animals, and a few wells, I noticed what appeared to be a great bank of fog, moving towards us from the southward. The Egyptian interpreter who rode in my car cried out that it was a sandstorm, and we ran the cars quickly to the lee side of the fort, while a violent wind arose and swept the swirling sand about us, until nothing could be seen at the distance of a yard. Breathing was almost impossible, and the darkness was eerie, while the grains of sand which were continually whipped against our hands and faces by the hot wind stung like the points of needles. We drew heavy tarpaulins over the cars, and secured them with ropes, but the force of the wind was such that it seemed as though it would blow the armoured vehicles right over. For nearly four hours I lay with my hands over my face, as a protection from the cutting grit. At the end of that time the dust pall lifted somewhat, and then we ran to the sea, a mile away and, stripping off our clothes, plunged in.

Chapter Three
The Advance On Sollum

By 7th March all arrangements had been made for the final move along the coast to Bakbak, and from there to Sollum. On that day General Peyton and his staff arrived at Sidi Barrani, and all the troops became more busy than ever with their preparations for the advance. I made ready two spare wheels in case of tyre trouble, and did some adjustments to my car. That night another terrific sandstorm sprang up, and so violent was the wind that I found it impossible to stand upright without holding on to something firm.

Two days later General Lukin with the infantry, including a brigade of South African troops, advanced unopposed to Bakbak, about half-way to Sollum. From there he was to turn south-west to the wells of Augarin, which lay close under the plateau called Haggag Sollum. The cliffs of this plateau rose in the desert twenty-five miles south of Sidi Barrani, and converged in a straight line on the sea coast, which they joined at the Bay of Sollum. The Khedival motor road proceeded along the shore to Sollum, but as it was thought that the plateau would probably be held by the enemy, a plan had been worked out for the final advance on the town to be carried out on the high ground. The faster and more powerful of the cars were to proceed direct from Sidi Barrani across the desert to one of the passes in the cliff.

Having reached the top, they were to turn north-west and proceed along the crest to meet the infantry, who would come up from the Augarin wells by the passes of Madyan and Aragib. The heavier cars and all the transport were to proceed slowly by the coast road, General Peyton marching with them.

On 10th March one of our cars was sent out to survey the ground, but it was caught in a sandstorm, and the driver hit a rock with his steering drop-arm. This accident prevented him getting very far. However, on the 11th, having shovelled away the great drifts of sand which the storm of the previous night had piled against our cars, we set out. In spite of rough going we managed to reach the foot of the cliff without any mishap, and there a halt was made and a brief survey carried out of the steep pass up which we now had to climb. When our route had been decided upon everybody set about the task of clearing away the loose stones and pieces of rock, so as to make some sort of clear path for our wheels.

Three Armoured Cars Ready For Action.

My car had reached the cliff at the head of the column, and accordingly I had the pleasure of making the first attempt to climb the pass, on ground which no wheels, except possibly some belonging to the Romans, had ever passed over before.

The rest of the drivers and gunners stood by, shouting cries of encouragement, as 'Blast' lurched, bumped and pitched over the rough ground. Already I was using the gear-box freely, from bottom gear to third, so as to gain a little extra momentum; second, third; now back again to bottom in the nick of time to save the engine stalling. 'Good old girl!' I muttered. 'Stick it! We'll get up yet!' Slowly she climbed, sometimes sideways like a crab, sometimes staggering this way and that like a drunken creature, but always going on, foot by foot nearing the top of the pass. Suddenly, with a last gasp, we came on level ground, and amid the cheering of the men at the bottom one of my tires burst with a bang. Fortunately it was on one of the double rear wheels, and I could proceed without changing it then and there. One by one the other cars crawled up, groaning, to the top, some of them being helped by a party of men pushing behind.

A few miles further along the plateau we made our camp for the night, as we had no wish to reach our place of rendezvous with the infantry a long time before they were due there. Guards were posted, with machine guns mounted on tripods, and the signallers were ready throughout the night with their flash lamps to answer any message signalled from the plain below.

Before dawn we were all astir, and as the first light came into the sky the column, led still by 'Blast,' proceeded on its way. I drove as close as possible to the edge of the precipice, picking my way between the great stones, and stopping frequently when further movement was made impossible by the obstructions. Then men from the other cars would run forward and remove some of the stones, until a passage had been opened large enough to drive through. For mile after mile we carried on in this manner, sometimes being forced to turn away from the cliff for a considerable distance in order to avoid a deep gully. Many of these gaps were so steep that they might have been cut with a huge axe in the side of the mountain.

When we had gone fourteen miles on this nerve racking journey a halt was called, and I received the order to drive as close as possible to the edge of a ravine so that the signaller whom I carried might set up his heliograph and try to get into communication with the troops advancing across the plain below. The Duke of Westminster watched anxiously as the call signal was flashed over the valley. Our eyes, straining to catch an answering flash, at last distinguished an intermittent glitter far away in the distant haze. All crowded round while the signaller repeated the letters: 'This is General Lukin. Left Bakbak early this morning. General Peyton then at point four miles east. Wells here almost dry. Searching for water. Position serious.' We had made contact with the infantry at Augarin, but their news was not encouraging. We could only signal back that we had as yet discovered no water on the plateau, and that our engines were boiling their water away at an alarming rate.

Proceeding on our way after this halt, we presently overtook two ancient Bedouins, a man and a woman. The woman ran away in fright, but the man was stopped and questioned. He informed the interpreter that the enemy had destroyed all the wells in the neighbourhood. This was alarming news, for our fantassis - metal tanks containing twelve gallons, and oblong in shape so that one of them could be conveniently slung on each side of a camel's saddle - were already nearly empty, the engines having boiled away large quantities. Our own ration was one bottleful a day for each man, and the heat of the atmosphere was such that the water came hot out of the fantassis. We had been informed that any man who attempted to take water from the radiator of a car or from the rubber bottle kept for the Maxim gun would be placed under open arrest and tried by court martial.

At last we came to the Madyan Pass, just as the first of the South Africans began to appear on the top of the plateau. And

30

what a meeting it was! I now witnessed scenes the most tragic, I think, that I had ever beheld. As soon as we had halted the men of the South African battalions stumbled towards us hurriedly and unsteadily, gasping out, 'Water! Water! For the love of God, water!' Their tongues hung out of their gaping mouths, as though they were seeking to touch something cool with them. The information concerning the water supply at Augarin, given to General Peyton by the intelligence agents, had proved to be unreliable; but he had insisted on keeping to his original plan.

Flesh and blood could not stand this sight, and all thought of our orders was promptly forgotten. Every drop of water we carried with us was shared out amongst these wretched men; but long after it had all gone, others, and still others, came straining over the edge of the cruel precipice and stumbling towards us, crying like babies and gesticulating like madmen, that we should keep just a few drops until they could drag their tortured bodies to where we had halted. A man would have given his heart's blood to help those famished men to get a little ease, but we had done all we could, and might do no more. No words of mine can give any idea of the horror of our situation, of our agony of helplessness as we watched these men visibly wilting and dying before our eyes.

One among many poor fellows who tore at my tunic with claw-like hands, and implored me to save him, pulled my head down to his mouth and whispered in my ear with his remnant of a voice, 'Look! Here is my card. I will write you an I.O.U. for any amount you like to mention. The money's safe. See! Fifty pounds for a drop of water!' He fumbled out his pay-book and took from it a card, frayed and dirty with being carried about on service. I glanced at it and saw his name, and underneath was written, 'Manager, National Bank, Cape Town.' I looked round me in despair; there was now no water except the boiling stuff in the radiators, and that in the sacred bottle belonging to the Maxim guns. 'My poor chap! I don't want your money,' I cried. 'I'd only be too glad to give you some water if I had any.'

Suddenly a new thought flashed into my mind. 'Wait a minute!' I said to the bank manager. I had remembered that the gunner of my car had kept an old rubber bottle, after he had been issued with a new one. That disused bottle had been thrown into my tool locker, and I thought it was just possible that a little water had been left in it. I went quickly and got the bottle, but when I unscrewed the stopper I was met by a putrid smell. I turned back towards the man as I began to screw in the stopper again, 'You can't drink this,' I said, 'it stinks.' But before I had finished speaking he had snatched the bottle from my hand and was gulping down its contents. 'Steady,' I said, trying to pull it away from him, 'you'll kill yourself.'

But the bottle would not come free of his vice-like grip, and all I could do was to wait until he had done. As soon as he had finished he dropped it and seized both my hands in his, looking in my face with eyes which blazed with gratitude, and begging me again and again to write to him after the war, if we were not able to meet again on this campaign. (After the war I did write, but I heard from a relative of his who replied to my letter that he had been killed in action on another front.)

These men whom we met on the plateau had broken away from their column in the plain below on learning that we were at the top of the cliff, being desperate with thirst. Early on the next morning General Lukin, having sent some of his troops back to General Peyton, advanced on to the plateau with the remainder, and we proceeded ahead of them to the wells of Siwiat, where we found some water.

At dawn the next day, 14th March, the battery moved forward, followed by the brigade of South African infantry and a mountain-gun battery. I was sent in advance as a scout, and after a short drive I came to the pass of Halfia, known to the troops as Hellfire Pass, where we had been ordered to halt and join up with General Peyton's column. This point was only about three miles from Sollum, and as we had filled all our water containers at Siwiat we felt ready and willing to exchange compliments with the enemy. Some more of our troops came up the Hellfire Pass to join our column, and then all advanced on Sollum. But the enemy had already left, and we marched into the town without firing a shot.

The cavalry took charge of Sollum, and the Armoured Car Battery was ordered to proceed to Bir Wair, two miles to the west. The orders given to the Duke were that he was to pursue the enemy, who were reported by the aircraft to be evacuating the place. When we got there we found their camp-fires still burning, but the men had gone. Excitement grew with every passing minute as we sped on to the westward, for the going was excellent, and we roared along sometimes at forty miles an hour. A lot of Bedouins were scattered about over the plain, but our orders from the Duke were to take no notice of these. We were after the Senussi regulars; as for the Bedouins, they always joined the side which they thought was going to win, so they might be considered as our friends now. Presently, however, I saw a fellow in trousers, and on overtaking him we found he was a Senusite. He willingly told us all about the flight of his comrades, and pointed out the direction they had taken, so we let him go, and proceeded.

About twenty-five miles out we came up with the Senusites, but they had chosen their ground well, and were scattering themselves over a stretch which was strewn with rocks. As soon as we came within range they opened fire on us with mountain guns and machine guns, but we charged straight at the gunners, as far as the rough ground would allow, spraying them with bullets as we went.

There were three of us in 'Blast' and, our movements being hampered by this overcrowding, we soon began to get irritable and snappy. The reek of burnt cordite, blending with the stench of our hot, sweating bodies, made us gasp for fresh air, but with the armour lid closed down there was little chance of getting any. The heat, a combination of that given out by the racing engine and that of the sun on the steel cylinder, added to the din of the stuttering gun and the clatter of the ammunition belts, made the conditions nerve-shattering. Hot, empty cartridge-cases frequently fell on my bare neck, and into my shirt, stinging my flesh; and the general sensation inside our war-chariot was infernal. My duties were to drive the car somehow, anyhow, as long as I got her forward, dodging the larger stones, which were difficult to see through the narrow slits, to find suitable targets for the gunner, bring the car into a position which would allow him to fire at them without sitting on my head, keep a keen eye on the enemy's gun positions so as to try to approach them without being hit, and frequently to drive with one hand while I fed the cartridge belt into the Maxim. The third man of us, an officer, acted as observer, peering out of the various apertures in turn and shouting orders at intervals, to turn right or turn left and make for such and such an objective. At the same time the gunner shouted to me to turn here or turn there towards something he had seen. Altogether I was very busy indeed, and in a state of mind between cursing and laughing.

A bullet found its way into our little fortress somehow, and hit the lieutenant's arm, but he went on urgently requesting me to turn left and turn right. So engrossed were we in our own affairs that we forgot all about the other fighting cars. They were in the same condition, and before long we were widely separated. The enemy had scattered, and their fire seemed to have ceased. Suddenly I shouted, 'There goes Nuri!'

The Turk was galloping away to the south-west like a streak of light on his beautiful piebald mare. Her long mane flew in his face as he bent low in his saddle, and her tail streamed out like a white plume. There was something fairylike about their figures, as they flew across the plain together, and for the moment they seemed unreal apparitions flitting in the grim desert. Suddenly I thought, 'Now for it!' and swinging the nose of my car towards the fast-receding rider, I gave chase. But what a run he gave us! He plunged at once into even more difficult ground, strewn thick with rocks. The excitement became intense as I strained every nerve to keep the car at the highest possible speed, and at the same time to avoid colliding with dangerous rocks. The other two continually urged me to greater speed. Yes, we were surely gaining on the wily Turk, and I could see him now and then turn his head to mark our progress. All the while I twisted and snatched the wheel this way and that, often missing the boulders by an inch or two.

Suddenly Nuri swerved more to the westward, and all but the top of his head disappeared behind a large rock. 'Get the gun ready!' I gasped. 'We'll have him yet.' For the moment we could no longer see anything of him, but in a minute or two more we came abreast of the rock and then we saw why he had turned off to his right. He had plunged into a belt of small dunes of shifting sand, and was rising and dipping in that heavy going, but maintaining a good speed. I looked quickly to the right and left to see whether we could get round the dunes on firm going and head him off, but Nuri had chosen his ground well; the soft sand extended on either side as far as I could see. I slipped her into low gear and charged the dunes with a terrific roar, spraying the sand in all directions. Slower and slower became our progress as the yielding sand sucked the life out of the engine, and gradually Nuri drew away from us. My radiator was boiling dangerously, and I began to feel that the time had come to give up the chase. However, I kept on grimly, and at last we struggled on to harder ground. But Nuri was now no more than a dot on the horizon. Suddenly there was a loud hang, and 'Blast' lurched clumsily. 'Burst tyre!' I gasped in response to the exclamations of the others; and we had to give

Nuri the palm. This was the second time he had escaped us after the defeat of his troops, and on both occasions I had to admire the skill of his getaway.

Having gathered our scattered wits we dressed the wound in the lieutenant's arm, changed the damaged wheel, and then began to return on our tracks. When we had got back across the sand dunes I increased speed, and soon we came to the scene of the action. Here we saw hundreds of dead and wounded Senusites lying on the ground, and there were numbers of prisoners standing about in straggling groups, looking ill-fed and unkempt in their ragged uniforms. Our ambulance men were busily engaged in giving first-aid to the seriously wounded; the dead were left to rot on the ground without ceremony. It was evident, though, that they would not remain there long enough to rot, for hungry vultures were already circling and screaming overhead.

We exchanged news eagerly with the fellows in the other cars as we lent a hand in collecting the spoil. There were three guns, nine machine guns, hundreds of rifles, about forty revolvers, and thousands of rounds of rifle ammunition. I took as my share a beautifully ornamented six-chambered automatic pistol, with a wallet full of ammunition. These I took from the dead body of a Turkish officer.

We made our camp that night near the scene of the battle, and though tired out with the strain and excitement we chatted and laughed unceasingly as we munched our bully beef and biscuits, exchanging our news, giving exaggerated accounts of what we had done, and roaring with laughter at the humorous episodes. Nearly all of us, it appeared, had been responsible for silencing Nuri's three guns; one fellow's shooting was so accurate that on taking aim at the seat of a pair of Senusite trousers he had whipped it clean away, so that the owner looked round in dismay, and then ran like a startled rabbit, with a white scut of shirt-tail hanging, gesticulating for courtesy with his hands as though in fear that the remainder of his garment would be as scientifically removed. Our two Canadians gave the best turn of the evening, however, but like so many amusing people, their conversation cannot be effectively relayed by anyone else. Amid roars of laughter they outdid one another with their far-fetched stories, and yet by their manner of speaking anyone who did not know them would have sworn that they themselves believed firmly that they were uttering nothing but spotless truth. The prolonged discussion in which they compared the merits of the Vancouver Navy and the Winnipeg Militia convulsed the whole camp to such an extent that it set everybody fighting for breath.

At last we sank to sleep in the moonlight through sheer exhaustion, all except the sentries, and the guard over the prisoners.

Chapter Four
The Rescue Of The Tara Prisoners

In the morning our departure for Sollum was delayed by swarms of our infantry who marched out to meet us, and who had to be told all about our doings of the day before. The sun was high by the time we, having handed our prisoners over to them, started off on our return to the town.

After covering about twenty miles at an easy speed we emerged from a belt of thick scrub, and then saw in the hazy distance the square fort of Sollum, standing out on its rock, above the Mediterranean. As we drew nearer the massive buttresses and square battlements became plainly visible, and with the blue background of the sea the whole scene was like a stage setting. This fort was to be our base for the future, and as we drove into the outer courtyard I already had a feeling as of homecoming. We drew up in an ordered line by the outer wall of the fort, for a messenger from the General Officer Commanding the force had informed us that we were to be inspected. We stood to attention beside our cars as General Peyton made his appearance. Having looked us over with an approving eye, he stood back and addressed us: 'Officers, Non-commissioned Officers, and Men of the Armoured Car Brigade! I congratulate you all on your splendid achievement. Nothing in the history of my command equals your gallant work of yesterday, and I thank you.' The order to dismiss was given just in time to save the buttons of our tunics from flying off as our breasts expanded with pride, and we rushed away to make our own inspection of our new quarters. In the middle of the courtyard we found a well in which a dead camel had been deposited some days before; the rooms in the building were strewn with vile filth and were in a ruinous condition; and the stench which met us everywhere was terrifying.

We lost no time in hoisting the Union Jack, and being all lined up on parade, the order was given and the guns began to crash out a salute. This was all very fine, especially as live shell was used; but unfortunately the gunners seemed to feel the necessity for a target and they aimed at us. The parade scattered and fled.

In the afternoon our prisoners, worn out and footsore, with their eyes sunk deep in their heads, and looking like a gang of convicts from Devil's Island, stumbled into Sollum, surrounded by their escort. They glanced this way and that with their famished eyes, looking for food, water and a place in which to rest their suffering bodies. First of all they were searched, and each man was closely interrogated. One old man, an Arab, was questioned more closely than the others, and placed apart under a separate guard. Later we learnt that a letter in English had been found in the possession of one of the inhabitants of Sollum. It had been sent by Captain Gwatkin-Williams, R.N., the officer commanding the gunboat Tara, to the commandant of the British garrison at Sollum; but unknown to him the British had withdrawn before its arrival. The old Arab amongst the prisoners had given information of the present whereabouts of Captain Gwatkin-Williams and the rest of the British captives held by the Senusites.

Over four months had now elapsed since the survivors from the torpedoed ship had been handed over by the German submarine commander to the Arabs, and all the attempts to induce Ahmed Es Senussi to order them to be given up had failed. There were about a hundred of them, and it was supposed that they were continually moved from place to place, for their whereabouts, as stated by our Arab agents and by Senusite prisoners, had never been confirmed. Aircraft pilots had reported sighting men who appeared to be the Tara prisoners, but further investigation had not confirmed these reports. The desert is a fastness to those who know it, and a cemetery to those who do not. What the condition of those unfortunate men could be by this time we could only guess.

According to the old Arab, Ali by name, the English prisoners were then at a place called Bir Hakim, over a hundred miles to the west of Sollum; and as soon as the Duke of Westminster understood that the information seemed reliable he volunteered to make a dash to the place with cars. Certainly old Ali did not suffer from a lack of speech, but how much of his cackle consisted of information I could not judge. He raised his eyes and hands to heaven, smote his breast, spoke sternly, meekly, pathetically, fiercely, and seemed anxious to keep us interested all day. From the interpreter we gathered that Ali himself had paid a visit to Bir Hakim, but it had been many years ago, in the days of his youth, when he was in charge of a flock of sheep. His old wizened face worked, and his old eyes blazed as he spoke of the distance, calculating the number of camel journeys which lay between us and our goal, his old fossilized mind apparently oblivious of the powers of the cars which stood parked all round us and which he himself must have seen in action.

Bir Hakim was reckoned to be about a hundred and twenty miles away, so we laid aboard our petrol accordingly, allowing a liberal margin. Extra rations of bully beef, biscuits, and tinned milk were put aboard for feeding those starved men. The various preparations occupied us all day on 16th March, for the column was to consist of forty-five cars in all, including armoured cars, tenders and ambulances.

In the earliest hour of the 17th, soon after midnight, we were aroused by the sentries, and at once the courtyard began to hum with voices and the movements of men. Light was supplied by the dimmed lamps of some of the cars, and by bits of candle. I had thrown a tarpaulin over my engine to protect it from the cold dew and so avoid difficulty in starting. The first turn of my crank handle produced a gentle purring, announcing that 'Blast' was ready for her journey into the unknown.

A Halt En Route. Derna Road, Tripoli.

With Esmi, the Egyptian interpreter, and old Ali as passengers, I led the column, being followed by the rest of the armoured cars, the Ford supply tenders and the ambulances. We skirted Bir Wair, and soon afterwards struck the road to Derna, a small town two hundred miles along the coast. Ali sat on the tool-box which was placed against the rear armour doors, huddled in the deep folds of his coarse clothing, and looking rather like a bale of old sacking. His wrinkled face peered out from under his headcloth. Esmi sat beside me, closely wrapped in his great-coat, for the air was chilly. Ali muttered some words to the interpreter, and the latter informed me that he was making a comparison between the ease of riding in a car and on a camel. This was his first experience of the former, and he was favourably impressed. I said to Esmi, 'Tell him to keep his remarks till he has been sitting on that tool box for a few more hours. He'll have a different tale to tell then.'

A halt was called for breakfast, and the bully beef and biscuits, and the hot tea tasted good after our drive in the cold air. There had been no mishap so far, and the column had kept well together. Drawn up behind the armoured cars were the light Fords, loaded with petrol, water and provisions, and behind these again the ambulances were strung out in a long line. Two armoured cars brought up the rear.

Our halt was short, and soon we were on the move again, following the Derna road and putting on speed wherever the going was firm and smooth enough to allow it. Nothing broke the monotony of the undulating plain but hills of sand or rock, grim and bare under the rays of the sun. Ali frequently rose to his feet now as though his seat was becoming uncomfortable; and he continually muttered, 'Yalla! Yalla!' which I knew meant, 'Go on! Go on!' I obeyed his directions for mile after mile, saying nothing to my companions, and staring ahead all the while, keeping a tense look-out for a group of starving British sailors. Would we find them lying about on the open desert, like men marooned after a shipwreck, or should we find them in Arab tents or in some sort of building, or in a cave?

Suddenly old Ali was on his feet again. 'Stanna! Stanna!' he cried. This meant 'Stop!' so I brought her to a standstill. We had covered about fifty miles. A great change had taken place in Ali; something had at last attracted his attention in the desert ahead, but I could see nothing there. He gazed out over the rocks and sand for some long minutes, without saying a word; and then, as though at last sure of his suspicions, he pointed with two long, bony fingers. Watching his face I saw a faint quivering of its muscles and a twitching of his nostrils, as though he were a greyhound held in leash. He said, 'Shuf!' and we both looked, but saw nothing. He said, 'Shuf!' and we both looked again, but still saw nothing. The Duke came up with his, powerful glasses and looked too; but neither could he see anything. Ali now began to get excited. We looked at Esmi, expecting him to produce a solution of the old man's capers.

Said the Egyptian, 'He says he can see a camel caravan, laden with goods. He knows they are for the Senussi.' Ali was now pouring out a spate of guttural Arabic at the interpreter, gesticulating violently at the Duke and me all the while. Esmi presently said with becoming modesty, 'He says the English are blind. They have eyes in their heads, but they see nothing. They have ears too, but they cannot understand plain speech.' Ali continued to give us a supply of plain speech, but, as he said, ears we had, but of understanding none.

The Duke gave the order to the armoured cars to go and investigate the mystery; so leaving the column halted where it was we swung off the track and moved away towards the south. We had not gone far under Ali's direction when, sure enough, we came in sight of a string of camels moving into the desert in the same direction which we were taking. Putting on speed we rapidly overtook them, and fired a burst from a machine gun over their heads. This halted them at once, and the men stood or sat on their camels with their hands held above their heads. On searching their loads we could find nothing connecting them with the Senussi, until suddenly somebody came across a Turkish field service book. The chief of the Arabs said they had found it lying on the ground, but Ali, keeping out of sight of the men as far as he was able, informed us that they were carrying supplies to the Senusites. He said he knew what he was talking about for he himself had been engaged in the same occupation. Having this valuable authority to base our actions upon, we forthwith confiscated all the goods, took the men prisoners, and shot their camels. My share of the plunder was a pair of Turkish slippers and a cake of soap. A cake of soap! This alone seemed sufficient evidence that they were in direct communication not only with the Turks, but with the

Germans.

We had already spent a good deal of valuable time on this little incident, so we hastened now to return to the main column. The men in the tenders and ambulances had meanwhile been watching our movements through their field glasses.

It was now nearly midday, and no further time was to be lost if we were to finish our mission in one day as had been planned. The prisoners and loot were loaded on some of the tenders and placed under guard, and then we pushed on. Bursts of speed were made now at every possible opportunity in the effort to make up some of our lost time. Esmi questioned old Ali repeatedly, pointing out to him the great truth that motor cars do not carry five days' supply of petrol in their bellies after the manner of camels. We had already come a hundred miles, and the Egyptian was beginning to feel the weight of his responsibility. But Ali's only reply now to all questions and admonitions was a majestic wave of his bony hand, sometimes accompanied by a grunt of disgust, as though he was indignant that anyone should question his knowledge of anything connected with the desert. Mile after mile flew by, as I drove on with a waiting mind; and then, quite suddenly, the old Arab gave the word to turn off the road, and drive into the desert to the southward, across country strewn with rocks and loose stones. I obeyed his directions mechanically, but I was shaken out of my doze; the atmosphere in my car seemed changed, and it was at this point that I began to seriously doubt Ali's knowledge or his good faith, or perhaps both.

Having left the road, although it was only a rough track, we now felt all at sea; and the Duke began to call frequent halts in order that we might discuss the situation between ourselves, with the aid of our guide. But the latter's reply to all our questionings was always the same - 'Go on, go on, go on!' The old man's confidence in himself seemed to be unshaken, but we had begun to feel that it was the confidence of ignorance or cunning, and our doubt in him increased with every added mile. Was this fellow leading us, ignorant of the desert as we were, into some cunning trap which had been carefully prepared for us by crafty, fanatical brains? Thoughts like this worried us continually, and our uneasiness increased as we faltered doubtfully onwards. We still kept up a good pace wherever possible, but our bursts of speed were now made grimly, not with the enthusiasm of the morning. True, the old man was our prisoner, but the stake was so large - all the honour and reward of delivering up to the Senussi a whole squadron of mobile forts - that it was quite possible that he had nerved himself to take the risk of not being able to slip out of our clutches when we ourselves had been safely entrapped.

No doubt, even without the aid of the interpreter, Ali knew that our faith in him was waning fast, for at every stop now he jumped down and threw himself on his knees in the sand, rasping out either prayers for guidance or else oaths in support of his knowledge and good faith. Esmi appeared to accuse him with our unspoken accusations, and this caused a violent argument between them. But old Ali, we gathered, was more determined than ever that we should go on. He smote his breast now, and beat his poor old head on the ground, as a sign of the whiteness of his heart, and the purity of his intentions. This demonstration of honesty impressed us a little, and the Duke gave the order to proceed still. And proceed we did until our sweat-stiffened shirts chafed us raw.

The day dragged on and the heat of the early afternoon was terrible. At every halt now there were open murmurings of the fruitlessness of our going on. Disappointment was plainly expressed on every tired face, and tempers were becoming ruffled with the strain of breaking hopes. 'This man's a fool!' said the Duke tersely. But the more we doubted the keener old Ali became. Like a bloodhound warming to the scent, he kept

45

his nose to the front, as it were, and pointing frantically ahead, cried again and again, 'Yalla! Yalla! Yalla!'

Now once more a halt was called, and this time the order came that we were to rest as far as possible before turning back for camp. We had come one hundred and fifty miles from Sollum. But we were not quite beaten yet, for although that order had been given, we had not yet moved off on the return journey, and I believe we felt subconsciously that the effect on us of taking a rest would be that when we got up again and mounted to our places the order would still be 'Forward!' Our rest was cut short very suddenly.

Survivors From H.M.S. Tara.

'He says he can see Bir Hakim!' an excited voice screamed out. It was Esmi. We had wearily left the interpreter and the guide to rasp their interminable repetitions at one another, and now as we looked at them with startled eyes I, for one, felt that we were indeed in sight of our goal. Somebody said, 'He's been seeing things all day.'

But the old man was running away across the sand with his rags flapping round his legs. 'He says he can see something,' cried Esmi again. 'Yes. Look! Look!' He, at least, was converted. We sprang to our feet, the Duke seizing his glasses. After a breathless moment he said doubtfully that the only objects visible were two small lumps on the sky-line. 'That is the place. That is what he says. That is Bir Hakim! Those are the two wells!' cried Esmi.

The order was given and the armoured cars moved ahead to investigate, leaving the rest where they were. Those two objects on the skyline slowly increased in size, and presently I could see things like flies running over the top of them. I felt at once that we had made no mistake this time, and scarcely had this conviction seized me when bullets began striking against the armour-plate of my car. The old man had not played us false.

My gunner had his weapon ready for action and I let 'Blast' out with a roar and raced over the hummocky ground, pitching, bumping, sometimes flying in the air, but going right at those two mounds. The other cars had deployed, and some of them were racing abreast of me. As we closed on the place the enemy ran out and scattered in flight over the desert. We gave chase, but all held our fire now, for we could see that there were others besides Senusites in that scattered crowd. They were trying to take some of their prisoners with them, the British sailors. We charged right up to the well mounds, and before we had halted we were surrounded on all sides by a throng of living skeletons. They were clad in old burnouses, rice sacks and the tattered remains of blue uniforms, and they spoke to us with breaking voices in the English tongue. Then there was no room left in us for compassion. We fended them off with firm and hasty hands; the engines roared, and we shot away after the creatures who had had it in their power to turn our fellow-countrymen into whimpering scarecrows, if only whimpering to us. The guards were running with their women and children, running for their lives. We did not look to see who or what they were - this was no politicians' game; at last we had something really worth fighting for. Men, women, and even children were mown down ruthlessly by our guns, in that mad hustle for revenge. I believe the only survivors were two little babies, picked up by somebody and brought back to the wells. We drove back there.

Of course it was all a mistake, as such things usually are. The Senussi had not ill-treated their prisoners as they understood treatment. These desert people starve every day of their lives, according to our notions of feeding. They had given their prisoners what they had themselves, and treated them decently, according to their own notions. It was beyond their power to do more. But it was a long time before I understood this. As they were ignorant of our ways, so we were ignorant of theirs; and that and the lust of grab are the cause of all the world's misery.

We did not understand. Here is what was written afterwards by one of those who were in the best position to understand:

'The armoured cars dashed off round the mound to reconnoitre. Almost immediately, while the Duke was questioning me as to our treatment, I heard the Maxims splutter. I shouted, "Save them. They have been kind to us," and dashed up the old well mound for the last time, the Duke with me. But we were too late, the garrison had been wiped out in a few seconds, and I could see only prostrate forms lying amongst the desert scrub. Unhappily, with them perished many women and children, who had run out with the soldiers.... Our guards had died like the brave Arabs they were, with arms in their hands, and "In death they were not divided."' ★

On our return to the well we were met by heart-rending scenes. Men, Englishmen, swarmed into my car and hugged

★ *In the Hands of the Senussi, by Captain R. Gwatkin-Williams, R.N., pp. 105-6.*

and even kissed me. I have never before or since seen men in such a state. 'Food!' they cried, 'Food!' I tore open my locker and tipped out my emergency rations of bully beef, and in their ravenous haste to get at the contents they ripped the tins open with their teeth. We knew well enough that many of them must be suffering with dysentery and other diseases, but it was impossible to refuse them. Biscuits and beef they ate in great choking mouthfuls, and they drank condensed milk straight out of the tins. The Duke boarded the fastest car and sped back to report our success to headquarters; and as soon as the ravening men had satisfied the sharp pangs of their hunger, and Gwatkin-Williams, the captain of the Tara, had numbered them, we packed them into the ambulances, which in the meantime had moved up and joined us. They numbered eighty-nine men; four others had died of their privations and been buried in the desert, and two had been sent north by the Senussi, where they were later surrendered to the Italians at Tabrouk.

The sun was dipping to the western plains as our convoy started on its long trek back to Sollum, and our men, too, showed signs of the strain, not only of this long day's journey, but of the fatigues of the past week. I led the way in 'Blast,' and my passengers now were one of our lieutenants and Captain Gwatkin-Williams. They both sat by my side, squeezed together in the gunner's sling.

Before we had boarded my car Gwatkin-Williams had taken me for a little walk so as to show me how the prisoners had managed to eke out the small rations which the Senusites had given them, for it appears that latterly their guards themselves had been reduced nearly to starvation point after the defeats that we had inflicted on their forces at Wadi Majid, Agagia, and Bir Wair. 'See here!' said he, stopping in his walk and pointing to the barren ground. I looked, but could see nothing but sand and rock anywhere. 'Watch this!' he said again, stooping down with an old penknife in his hand, 'Look! This little weed!'

Yes, there was a little weed growing there. He scraped away the sand and pulled it up. Then from the root he extracted a small kernel. 'Eat this!' said he, handing it to me. A wan smile lit up in his face as he watched my expression change, for I found the kernel sweet and told him so. Then he led me a little further, and presently kicked away a loose stone. I saw some white snails under it. As he cracked one of these with a stone and took out the slimy contents and offered it to me I shuddered with disgust. But he smiled again and put it in his mouth. 'What! Eat that!' I exclaimed. 'Why, yes,' said he. 'Just as good as a small oyster.' I watched him in astonishment. 'Yes,' he said, 'we've lived on little else but these morsels for weeks. I've kept my boys alive with them, at least the majority of them. But dysentery was gradually getting us down. Most of us have it to some extent. There was no medicine. We kept on hoping against hope that something would be done to rescue us, but it seemed as though that hope was never going to be realized.'

Now in the car he began to tell his story in rambling fashion as I drove towards Sollum at the head of the column. 'I made my escape from Bir Hakim,' he said, 'on a moonless night. At first I kept on running as fast as I could manage, trying to keep towards one direction. Those fellows can see an enormous distance, and I wanted to get out of sight before dawn. I managed this, and then went on, travelling at night with the help of the stars, and sleeping under whatever cover I could find by day. I lived on a small supply of rice, ready boiled, and bread, which I had hoarded up, and which I carried in the legs of my cotton trousers. I drank sparingly from my waterskin, which at starting contained about a gallon and a half. My greatest fear was that I might fall in with Bedouins, who, I had no doubt, would give me up to the Senussi in the hope of getting a reward. I managed to get almost within sight of Sollum, which I thought was still occupied by our fellows. But in reality the Senusites had had it for weeks. In the end I was recaptured by Bedouins, as I had feared, and handed over to two Senusites, who took me back to Bir Hakim by a roundabout way.'

So he rambled on, like a man in a trance, occasionally relieving his terrible story with a touch of humour. The interest of his tale helped to keep my drowsy senses from falling asleep. I frequently came out of a doze with a start, and found that he had given me a nudge, and was still repeating his anecdotes in the effort to keep me awake. Sometimes I fell against him with the jolting of the car, and still he went on talking of his experiences. I learnt later that he had had a good deal of practice in story-telling during the past four months, for it was one of the methods which he and his fellow-officers had used for keeping up the spirits of their men. They all swore by him, and had a great affection for him for the way in which he had tended the sick and the dying, doing all he could to alleviate their sufferings.

On and on we drove. Night had fallen long since, and still we kept moving in the darkness. I was hardly conscious of anything now, but I kept the car moving by a mechanical control of my limbs. I had to use my eyes as well, however, and presently, as the hours still crawled by, I was obliged to use one hand to hold my eyelids open. My arm ached agonizingly with the strain of this, until at last it seemed to become fixed so as to no longer require much exertion to keep it raised. Gwatkin-William's voice went on all the time, the car lurched and bumped, the wheel slipped from my hand, I grabbed it again, and again knew nothing. Then voices were shouting somewhere, and lights were flashing in front of the car. I suppose I stopped the car. I heard the twanging voices of Australians. Somebody said, 'Bir Wair.' I sank down in a heap in my sling, and was at rest.

When I awoke there was a dim diffused light in the car, but

the air was stuffy and very hot. There was no sound of men, but only a howling wind. This perplexed me, and I raised myself on one elbow and lifted the flap of a rifle aperture. A little stream of sand poured through the hole. Then I found that I was lying in a bed of sand, which had blown into the car. Evidently there was a sandstorm raging outside. I tried once to open the door, but found it blocked by a sand drift on the outside, so I left it alone. Then I heard voices, evidently coming from other cars; and comforted by the sounds I drew my blanket over my head, rolled over, and went to sleep again.

At some time or other I was again awakened, this time by a crash on the armour doors, and a voice shouting, 'Let me come in!' I told him to come right in, whoever it was; and after a struggle my gunner managed to open the door wide enough to squeeze in. He carried in his hands two tins of bully beef, which was a cheering sight, for I was ravenously hungry. As we ate he told me that we had drawn the cars up in a circle on the night before at Bir Wair, where we now were, helped by some of the Australian Camel Corps, who had formed an outpost here. One of them with a light had helped him to get me out of my sling, and he had then laid me out on the floor of the car and thrown a blanket over me. It was now afternoon, he said, and the ambulances had taken the Tara boys into Sollum.

The storm lasted two whole days, and on the third we dug out the cars and drove to the fort. After two days of semi-darkness the bright sunlight made real holiday weather. The white fort was lit brilliantly and looked more like an enchanted castle than ever. Infantry cheered us as we drove through the wire entanglements, and a gun began to boom. We drove into our courtyard and took station in line before the western wall. There was to be another inspection by the General.

Begrimed and ragged, we lined up in front of the cars. 'Shun!' came the order, and we tried to click our heels as they do in well-behaved armies. The Old Man, that is General

52

Peyton, had got his matter written out on a paper. Again we heard proudly that nothing like this had ever been done before in the whole history of his command. The Duke of Westminster was to be recommended for suitable decorations in recognition of his daring leadership. He had taken his unit into an unknown desert to effect a most daring rescue, which would go down in military history as an outstanding achievement. The officers, non-commissioned officers and men under his command had performed their duties with equal skill and courage, and they too would be recommended to the proper quarter for suitable recognition.

In Sollum we saw our rescued sailors again. They were now wearing blue hospital clothes, and we were able to shake hands with them, exchange promises to write, and so on, before they got on the camels which were to take them down to the beach. From there they embarked in a hospital ship which lay in the bay.

Chapter Five
In Hospital

The fort of Sollum was situated at the top of the cliffs which overlooked the port, and which formed the edge of the westerly plateau. Its garrison, therefore, had the task of protecting the town from attack by enemy forces coming out of the high desert. One battery of four armoured cars was now detailed to form part of the permanent garrison at this point; a second was given the duty of patrolling the lines of communication between it and Matruh, a distance of over one hundred and fifty miles; and the third was to return to Matruh itself and join the garrison of that base. My car belonged to the battery which was ordered to Matruh, and on 21st March we paraded for the journey.

Our first difficulty was to get the cars down the steep camel track which led from the top of the cliff to the plain. We had originally climbed on to the plateau by a comparatively easy pass at the inland end of the Hagag Mountains, forty miles south-east of Sollum, thus following two sides of a triangle in making our advance from Sidi Barrani; but now it was desired to use the shorter route, passing directly along the coast.

I was detailed to make the first attempt at the descent; and several long ropes having been tied to the rear part of 'Blast's' chassis, these were manned by some of my comrades, while others gently pushed my car towards the edge of the precipice. As the front wheels sank over the brink my mind began to review in furious haste a series of safety devices which I ought to have had about me, but had not; and prominent amongst these was a parachute! Further and further over I went, the floor of the car rising up behind me and sinking from under me, as though it was anxious to exchange places with the sling which no longer supported my back. The car was now in such a position that had my colleagues eased the strain on the ropes a little too much it must have crashed right over in a somersault. I was standing nearly upright on the brake-pedal, with the floor supporting my back. Slowly they let her creep down the cliff, but steering was only possible to a slight degree, and had to be done with the greatest caution. Soon we were held up by a rock against the front axle, and jacks and levers had to be brought into play by another gang of helpers. As the perilous descent continued confused shouts were uttered by this man and that, cries of warning, or approval, or relief. Some gave random orders, and contradicted themselves in the next breath, for the strains and stresses were so many that nobody could tell exactly what would happen as the result of any given movement.

Presently, however, as the ropes were slowly paid out, I came on ground which sloped less violently, and my progress became easier and more rapid, until at last I slid into the shallow sand at the bottom. From there I drove on without further difficulty to the hard road which followed the coast to Matruh, and once on this I halted to await the descent of the other cars of the battery. The scene, as I looked back, was magnificent. The bare, lofty mountains were closely grouped about the Bay of Sollum, as though to protect the little town and the transparent blue waters at their feet from the savage desert which swarmed almost up to their crests on the other side. Before the town the tents of our infantry were neatly ranged on either side of the Khedival road. Washing hung on lines rigged between them, or on the tent-ropes, shirts and socks flapping gaily in the breeze, and giving a pleasant touch of homeliness to the grim desert scene. To one side lines of tethered mules stood twitching their long ears, or making circular kicks, in an effort to drive away the flies.

When at last the complete battery, with its transport vehicles, was formed up on the road and ready to start for Matruh it was already past noon. The order was given without delay, and away we went in a cloud of dust, with the farewell shouts of the camp in our ears. The going was easy compared with most of that which we had had in the past, but as the cars sped along between sea and mountains there was a good deal of pitching and tossing, the surface of the well-worn road having been churned into dust in many places by mule carts and general service wagons. In order to avoid each other's dust the drivers strung themselves out at long intervals, so that the column stretched to a great distance, and appeared like a series of swiftly moving dust-clouds on the road.

Running on thus without pause we passed Bakbak as the sun sank to the mountain crests, turning the brown crags to gold; and by the time we reached Bir Shaibia the falling darkness made driving on the ill-defined road dangerous. Being anxious to make Sidi Barrani that night, however, we broke the rule against using lights. It was long since I had driven at night with headlights on, and it was a great comfort to have the powerful beam illuminating every object, so that after going a mile or two I could increase my pace almost to the speed which we had maintained during the daylight hours, though I now had in tow a Ford tender which had no lights of its own.

Arrived in our camp at Sidi Barrani, my gunner and I prepared to make ourselves comfortable for the night. We sat opposite each other in the steel cylinder, cross legged on the little square mats, and proceeded to make cocoa by the light of a small electric lamp. As we smoked and discussed the events of the day, a primus stove hissed and spluttered between my legs, with a mess-tin of water on it. The water coming to the boil, I said to my companion, 'Where's the cocoa?'

He said, 'Behind the gear-lever,' so I turned to my right to look for it, resting my elbow on the floor, while my left knee came towards the water-tin on the stove. Before I was aware of what was happening they had come in contact, and with a tinkling clatter the tin with its boiling contents was upset on my right ankle. I gave a yell, and struggled to tear off my boot and sock. The skin came off my ankle with the latter, and I looked at it with dismay and exasperation, fearing that I should now be ingloriously disabled and perhaps sent to hospital.

I managed to get my car to Matruh with the rest, but once in the camp there I found it necessary to use a stick to enable me to hobble about. It was a miserable ending to the adventures of the past sixteen months. In the evenings I made my way to the tent of a friendly corporal, and there we played chess, but I lost every game. At last, in spite of my assurances to the doctor that I was feeling much better, I was sent to bed in the canvas hospital. My ward was a small marquee with eight beds in it, and here, with seven others who were really ill, I lay counting the flies which crawled about the underside of the canvas roof in the terrific heat. The long afternoon passed away at last; night came, and a hurricane lamp was placed on a table in the centre of the tent, where its light caused strange shadows to move about the forms of my sleeping companions. Now and then I closed my eyes and settled myself to drop off to sleep, but I had been inactive for days and sleep would not come. Suddenly I became conscious of unexpected movements. I opened my eyelids languidly, expecting to see one of my fellow-patients getting out of his bed, but instead I saw close up at my bedside a white-clad form, and my eyes, running up this, came to rest on a face which in that dim light seemed too mysteriously beautiful to be human. A sweet voice murmured, 'Are you awake?' It was the night sister, whom I had not seen before, and I was too fascinated to speak. After living in a mob of cursing, foul-mouthed soldiers for over a year I had almost forgotten that human beings existed who were gentle and tender. This undegraded being seemed to be supernatural, and her extraordinary kindness seemed to raise one's hopes of attaining to a new kind of glory, gentle, clean and spiritual.

It was a joyful event to be awakened every morning by this girl and to hear her inquire, in her musical voice, how we all were. When we became humanly acquainted, which actually happened, though I should have thought it impossible on the night when she first appeared to me, I ventured to tell her my first impression of her. She replied to this with a merry peal of laughter, and for some time afterwards, whenever she caught my eye, she could not refrain from laughing.

Many visitors came to my bedside and helped to relieve the monotony of my existence by day, but my foot became worse and I suffered a good deal of pain. One man came almost daily, bringing his shaving gear with him, and made me facially presentable. My lieutenant brought me cigarettes and cordial wishes for my recovery, and in fact everybody showed me so much kindness and sympathy that I began to think I was ill.

But I dreaded the visits of the day sister. She always arrived with the medical officer, determined to exhibit my wound to him without a moment's delay. 'This is a case of burning, doctor,' she would say, as she began to unwind my bandage. The night angel always removed the actual dressing very gently, having first thoroughly soaked it in water; but this method was considered as unprofessional by the day sister. Her way was to seize the dry dressing with a vice-like grasp of her professional hand, and with one sharp snatch to wrench it away, making the blood flow. 'Never mind, laddie,' said the doctor fatuously; and when he had gone the sister would bring me three sweets as a sort of peace offering, but they tasted sour to me. She of the night had no need to bring bits of sweet trash in her hand.

After some time I discovered that three others from my battery were in a small tent near mine. I forget what their complaints were, but I saw at once that both they and I could help each other to get well again by joining forces. By cunning talk I managed so to work on the mind of the young doctor that he agreed to have me moved to their tent. I had found out that this medico was a bit of a fire-eater, and that he would have liked to be in the fighting line. He was never tired of listening to my stories of our campaign, and it was really in exchange for these that he had me moved.

Having a small marquee to ourselves, the four of us were able to set about making arrangements for getting well without fear of causing a relapse to anyone else. Visitors increased in numbers, but we had to have them in in relays, as our accommodation for guests was only enough for ten at a time. Some of them brought a portable gramophone, which they left with us; another brought an acetylene lamp for use after 'lights out'; a third brought a pack of cards. In fact, whatever we prescribed for the alleviation of our complaints seemed to be forthcoming. The medico, without anything more than a mild suggestion from us, prescribed bottles of stout and tinned chicken, and watched our improvement with a twinkle in his eye. Indeed, we worked out such a first-rate system that our healthy visitors began to show a desire to try its merits. 'I say, old chap, how do you manage to get in here?' one and another began to say to me. We were in such high spirits, and probably looked so well as the result of our treatment, that it must, indeed, have seemed to an outsider that we had 'got in' by subterfuge.

The medico often paid us unofficial visits, and one evening he came in elated after a drive of forty miles into the desert in one of the cars of our battery which had gone out on a patrol. It was plain that he had been thrilled by the experience and that he was longing to get posted to a fighting unit.

All went on very well for some time, but presently some unseen hand began to curtail the liberal treatment which we had prescribed for ourselves. My acetylene lamp was suddenly found to be missing, and our midnight card parties were seriously handicapped in consequence. The gramophone, too, was found tidied away in inaccessible places, and altogether the atmosphere of our tent began to lose its healthful gaiety. When we reported the handicaps to health which were being put in our way to one pretty sister she told us with blushes that she would not dream of taking a hand in anything so unkind. Eventually we fastened the blame on the bandage-snatcher, but there was no proof that she was responsible.

Another trial which befell us was caused by sand storms, some of which were so fierce that we feared for the safety of our tent, and the swirling sand covered our food before we could eat it. Hundreds of patients suffering from dysentery were brought into the hospital every day at this period, and for two days my own temperature rose considerably, so that the doctor reduced my diet to castor oil and arrowroot.

At last, on Good Friday, 21st April, I was discharged from the hospital, though I still remained an out patient and hobbled about clumsily in a state of convalescence. Just before the end of the month my battery left for the fort of Sollum again, where they were to do a spell of garrison duty. But although I was left behind as unfit for duty, I was not dismayed as I had made a valuable friend. He was the servant of an officer of the Matruh garrison, and he could be relied upon to produce tasty morsels from his master's kitchen. He suggested that we should take up our quarters in a stone block house, and a kindly sergeant of the R.A.M.C., who was leaving the place, presented me with his spring mattress. A wooden case which had once held tins of petrol served as a table, and for chairs we had ammunition-boxes. On the first night our dinner consisted of olives from a nearby grove, wild tomato, which was a weed in the desert, and a couple of sardines purloined from the larder of my friend's 'bloke,' as hors-d'oeuvre; soup made from meaty bones from the same source; stewed quail, which we had shot ourselves, quails abounding at this season; spaghetti and cheese done to a turn, with tomato sauce of our own manufacture;

tinned pineapple and condensed milk, and cafe au lait out of a bottle, served with Flag cigarettes as issued officially to His Majesty's Forces.

After this excellent meal in our desert block-house we sat back with a sigh of satisfaction and felt completely at peace in a war-racked world. Our larder was well supplied for the future, for our sergeant friend, whose hospital was being moved, brought us stores of several kinds which he was unable to carry with him, including tins of rolled oats and of condensed milk. Our household pet was a fine chameleon which I one day took off a clump of greenish scrub. I brought him home on the twig which he had been sitting on, and hung this from the ceiling with him still on it. His antics caused us great amusement, and we christened him Tiny, for he was only about eight inches long, including his tail. He clung all day long to the twig, with each of his brilliant eyes revolving independently of the other, as he watched the flies crawling on the ceiling. As soon as a fly came within range - almost, it seemed, as soon as it had formed the intention to come within range - Tiny's cheek would swell out and his mouth would open just a little so that the tip of his tongue could be seen, ready for action. Then, quicker than lightning, and far more smoothly, his tongue would shoot out like a dart and instantly recede into his mouth again with the fly adhering to its end.

Often my friend and I would take a Ford tender and go out to a well in the desert to get fresh water which had not been chlorinated, for that in the camp had been doctored to such an extent that it was undrinkable. On these excursions we sometimes rounded up two or three half-wild desert sheep and, having killed and dressed them, we took them back to camp with the water. On one occasion we came upon an old Roman well, and perched on a rock at its mouth there were two fine specimens of the desert owl. These birds were always very difficult to approach, and there was therefore some sport in stalking and shooting them. I left the car and crawled towards them on my hands and knees, frequently dropping on my chest and clutching my automatic pistol in one hand. I managed to get within twenty-five yards of them without putting them to flight, and then I fired. One bird fell to the ground, but as I had determined to get them both I stalked the other during the next three days. Finally I shot him too, as he was sitting on the same rock on which I had shot his mate.

The month of May came in and the heat of the Libyan summer was fully upon us. Our daily routine now included the picking of ticks off our blankets, and the bites of fleas and sometimes of lice often made us wake up cursing at night to grope for the tin of Keating's Powder. By this time I had recovered sufficiently to be subject to 'medicine and duty,' which meant that while still parading for a daily dose of tonic I was liable to be detailed for any kind of work, and that unless I could safely dodge it I should have to do it, as I could no longer plead that I was convalescent. Before long I was told off for guard duty, and this meant a great deal of preparation, since I had not looked at my rifle for months and the brass buttons on my tunic were black. It took me the whole of the preceding day to produce a polish in the inside of my rifle-barrel and on my buttons and boots.

We gathered outside the guard-room at 6 p.m., and there awaited the fog-horn sound of the garrison sergeant-major's order to fall in. As the officer of the guard approached the whole desert seemed to rumble with the worthy man's bellowings - 'Fall in, there! Dress by the right! Now then, smartly to it! Steady! . . GUARD! . . . 'SHUN!' Tense as a blown-up goatskin, the garrison sergeant-major salutes, his great red hand vibrating like a piece of struck rubber at the brim of his helmet. Orders are read; the new sentry exchanges place with the old; the rest of the guard are dismissed to the guard room, the same orders being repeated again and again for every little movement which is to be made by each Tommy Atkins. It all sounded very funny on the dignified desert, but soldiers will be soldiers, all the world over.

At nine o'clock I was mounted for my spell of duty. My orders were to march back and forth along a given beat in a soldierly manner, to challenge all doubtful objects, and to call out the whole guard on the slightest provocation. It was a very dark night, and I tramped to and fro for what seemed like hours, my feet aching and my rifle at the slope, or perhaps I should say at a slope, for 'the' slope requires more exertion than I was just then prepared to bestow on my expectant country.

Suddenly a head popped out of a block-house and a voice whispered, 'Say, here's a cup of cocoa!' It was getting chilly, and I thanked my benefactor sincerely for his kindness. Placing my rifle against the wall I proceeded to sip the cocoa, mentally thanking providence for this unexpected gift. I was about fifty yards from the guard-room.

Suddenly a voice bellowed, 'Turn out the guard!' I dropped the cocoa on the instant and moved on tiptoe towards the guard-room at the double.

'Where's the sentry?' demanded the voice.

'Here I am, sir!' I said smartly; and there I was.

The guard tumbled out, rubbing its sleepy eyes, and buckling on its side arms. The officer of the guard, he who had caused all the disturbance, now accused the sentry, that is me, of talking while on guard. This rash accusation I flatly denied, forgetting, in the confusion of the moment, that in practice, whatever official regulations may say about it, I was not entitled to reply to the remark of a superior officer unless my reply was in agreement with what he said. Without further ceremony I was placed under arrest, that panacea for all the spiritual or temperamental ills of soldiers.

I was duly charged with the wrong heinous crime, namely, of talking while on guard; whereas the heinous crime which I had actually committed was that of drinking a cup of cocoa while on guard. The officer had seen nothing, but he had heard the sound of voices somewhere in the dark. Mine was certainly not one of them, as I had not spoken for some minutes before his order to turn out the guard, and, moreover, I was then in the opposite direction to that from which he said the voices had come. But, of course, my word was nothing against his, and if I had called my benefactor to prove that I was drinking his cocoa, not only should I have been punished for drinking it, but he would have been punished as an accessory to the crime. The officer's conception of his duty apparently was not so much to do his bit to ensure that the guard was carried out efficiently as to strain every nerve to prove that it wasn't.

My punishment was to do two extra guards, to be carried out on the two nights following, to lose two days' pay, and to be severely lectured for talking by the captain who took my case. I was made to feel that as a soldier I was a 'wash-out,' and no doubt this would have improved my military qualities enormously, but fortunately I did not remain long enough in that rarefied atmosphere to make sure of this. I received notice to prepare to rejoin my battery at Sollum, and very gladly I responded. In the armoured car squadron ideas of discipline were not so childish as in the base camps run on infantry lines, and besides I was thoroughly sick of stagnation.

Three of us - a lieutenant, Esmi the interpreter, and I - boarded a little ship called the Misr late in the afternoon of 6th June, and so journeyed westward through the hot night. Throwing my ground-sheet and blanket on a hatch cover I lay down there and talked with Esmi far into the night.

Chapter Six
Sport

At sunrise the high mountains round the Bay of Sollum came in sight, and soon we could see the white fort on the crest, and the village nestling below. There was not a ripple on the clear blue water, and as we moved further in towards the shore we could see the rocks and sand of the bottom.

The first news that we heard on landing brought a feeling of dismay. H.M.S. Hampshire had been sunk off the Orkneys, with the loss of all aboard her, including Kitchener and his staff. A sense of gloom seemed to hang over the whole camp.

We found a tender belonging to the squadron and got into it, and soon were astonished to find ourselves speeding up a well-made road, which wound and twisted in sharp but well-graded bends to the top of the cliff. This was the work of the Egyptian Labour Corps, directed by British engineers, and excellent work it was; great quantities of rock had had to be blasted and cleared away before a beginning could be made on creating a level surface. The fort, too, was now transformed. On one side the ground outside the walls had been levelled in terraces, and on these rows of white tents were pitched, each with a line of whitewashed stones surrounding it. Each terrace was bounded in front by a low wall of stones, and stone-bordered paths ran from tent to tent. There was no longer any sign of the filth and disorder in which the Senusites had left the place. Later in the day I wandered off along goat paths to explore the mountain and find new viewpoints of the wonderful scene.

The next day we were startled by the garrison alarm signal.

The crews dashed to their cars; engines were cranked up, guns loaded, and away we shot, out of our compound, through the wire entanglements and into the open desert. I had rushed to my car with only one boot on and carrying the other in my hand, expecting to be in my place, with a few moments to spare, before the gunner had mounted his weapon. But he was as quick as I was. Somebody shouted 'Right away!' I banged 'Blast' into gear, operating the clutch with a bootless foot, and we were the first through the wire. How good it was to be handling again the car I knew so well!

In single file we moved to the north-west, searching in every watercourse and behind every rock for lurking foes, but there were none to be found; so we returned and reported accordingly.

The Italians had now established a post within forty miles of us, to the westward, and presently we were informed that the Italian general intended to pay us a visit. This caused a great deal of nonsensical fuss; our equipment, our quarters, and our clothing were put through a rigid inspection nearly every day. We were ordered to polish all brasswork, and make everything spick-and-span. The paintwork of the cars was touched up wherever it had been scraped or scratched and everything was done to improve their appearance.

On the appointed day the most highly polished of the armoured cars was sent to escort the Allied general into our midst, the driver being given strict instructions to lead the procession in by a way which gave the greatest impression of smartness. In the camp a guard of honour was formed of the smartest-looking men, and considerable ceremony was to be displayed by our officers, who were to be introduced one by one to the visitor, dressed in their best clothes, and shining like little suns as the result of overworking their unfortunate servants. Most of our gunners were smart and fine-looking men, who had been drawn from the machine-gun sections of crack cavalry regiments, and they knew how to make themselves outwardly immaculate in true professional style; but the drivers were temporary soldiers, and a mean-looking lot when it came to spit-and-polish. Accordingly, we were enjoined to keep discreetly on the opposite side of our cars to that on which the Italian general might happen to be, as far as possible; and no doubt the effect of this order was to make us look meaner than ever, not to say furtive.

All this had been carefully arranged, and the whole show dressed like a shop window, long before the little general in plumed hat and medal-spattered uniform alighted from his car at the saluting-base. He beamed benevolence on the gallant array of officers who stood stiffly, with hands to caps, to do him honour. As he proceeded to shake each of them by the hand, the gunners' guard gave him the general salute in the best Aldershot style, and we who lurked uneasily by the cars felt proud of them. After a short palaver with some of our officers the Italian walked towards the line of cars; worse than that, he walked straight at 'Blast.' He was a quick walker, by Jove! There he was already, standing in front of my car, pointing at it, and asking the Duke in French where the driver was! The driver was obeying orders strictly, keeping well out of sight at the rear of the car. However, fresh orders came on the instant, and out I had to step, as smartly and cheerfully as I could. The visitor asked me something in Italian, I guessed, so I replied in French that no, I could not speak Italian, but I knew a little French. This seemed to answer the purpose, for he began fussily to ask a few questions about the powers of my car. He was an excitable little man, it appeared, and did not always wait for the end of my rather halting replies, but I satisfied myself at least by giving answers to all his questions. I was amused to note that the guard of honour was looking rather disgusted at not having been thoroughly inspected, and they were glaring their contempt at me. My situation, in fact, was becoming a little complicated by the time His Excellency moved away. This was our worst experience, and I think we were all glad when it was over.

The midsummer heat was now intense; it seemed to beat down from the sky and rise up from the earth at the same time. During the middle hours of the day we were almost incapable of exertion, and just lay about limply, longing for the hour when the sun would slant down to the west, and allow us a little ease. One poor fellow in the camp below was so tormented by the climate that he shot himself dead, and there may have been others. Only when the sun sank did we feel relief, and in the cool of the evening we grew light-hearted again and our life seemed worth living. One of our favourite pastimes was shooting gazelle. These timid little beasts roamed in herds over the desert, but a hunter could only approach them when the wind was blowing in his face and there was plenty of cover for him to hide in as he crept towards them. The moment they saw or scented a man they were away like arrows, and gone from sight in a few moments. We found the best way to bag them was by using a Ford tender or two with machine guns mounted in them. The car would go out with its driver and gunner, and with two other men armed with rifles. As soon as a herd of gazelle was sighted the car was brought to a standstill, if possible behind cover, and the riflemen alighted. The latter would then creep stealthily towards the animals on their hands and knees, and while they were doing this the car would be driven away in a wide detour so as to get on the opposite side of the herd without disturbing it. The riflemen, if satisfied that they had come as close to the animals as they were likely to get without startling them, would then open fire on them in such a way as to drive them as near as possible to the car. As they passed, the gunner would let fly at them with his machine gun. With all this precaution we very rarely bagged more than two animals, even when the machine gunner was a first-class shot. Very often our exertions met with no reward whatever.

On one of these hunting expeditions two cars went out, carrying two days' rations for the occupants. They had to travel many miles before sighting a herd, but at last they succeeded. The excitement became so intense that they circled this way and that without keeping any sort of count of their movements, and before their chase was over they had lost sight of all familiar landmarks. They had no compass, and they had to drive by the aid of the sun till their petrol gave out. When they had been absent three days a search party was sent out to look for them. The rescuers, of whom I was one, managed to distinguish their tracks from many others which were older, and after following these in zigzags and circles for a great distance we at last sighted two specks on the horizon, and these proved to be the missing cars. The men in them had been badly frightened, fearing that they had gone beyond the reach of timely rescue and would remain marooned in the sands until overtaken by death.

A less adventurous form of sport, but a very popular one in that hot, dry climate was swimming in Sollum Bay. Our battery had its water-polo team, and with goals made with moored petrol cases many exciting matches were played. One member of the team threw the ball so powerfully that every time he hit a goal with it he smashed the wooden case to matchwood. I remember that one day my head happened to be in the line of one of his shots, and I almost lapsed into unconsciousness from the stinging force of the impact.

When not employed in hunting or swimming we sometimes did a little reconnaissance work in the desert, with the object of locating the remnants of the enemy's forces. These expeditions usually lasted four or five days, and the surrounding desert became well known to us as time went on. On one occasion we had travelled far to the south, and as our water was getting low we were keeping a sharp look-out for wells, but all those which we had passed were dry. Suddenly my gunner cried out that he could see a water-hole, so I turned in the direction which he indicated, and came to a stop near the supposed well. It was a square hole in the surface of the ground, about three feet across and edged with stone. I looked into it, but could see nothing, and when I spoke with my head over it the echoes of my words resounded weirdly. Other cars had now joined us, and their occupants crowded round the hole while I called for somebody to bring my rope. While we were lowering a lamp into the depths on the end of my rope, somebody called out that he had found another similar hole a little further away; and then another was found. The holes were about ten paces apart, and there seemed to be many of them in a small area. We went on lowering the light, but it grew dim in the depths without reaching the bottom. On clearing away the drifted sand for several yards round the hole, we found solid stone under it. I now dismounted my powerful head-lamp from 'Blast,' and shone it down into the well, and with the aid of its beam we thought we could see something which looked like a solid floor.

Several fellows volunteered to be lowered through the hole, and having selected the smallest and lightest of them we tied the rope in a loop so that he could sit in it, and let him down cautiously. When we had paid out about thirty feet of line something took the weight off, and the rope slackened in our hands. It was plain that our man had reached the bottom, and we could see his light moving sideways down there. Some of the others now began to have themselves lowered through the holes, and I descended among them. The place was like a gigantic stone hall, in the roof of which the square apertures appeared like small ventilators. It had certainly been used as a water cistern, and appeared to be a natural cave, though it had been squared to some extent, and the floor levelled. In Roman times this must have been one of the most important stations on the road from the coast to the Siwa Oasis.

My companions looked rather like ghosts of Roman soldiers, I thought, in the feeble light of our lamps, in spite of the fact that they cast shadows across the floor. The shadows themselves seemed not ordinary, as they flickered and wavered amongst the bones of men and animals, and the filth and rubbish, which lay everywhere. The feeling of mystery here was far deeper than that raised at the sight of the sunlit pyramids of Giza. But the job which we had in hand gave little opportunity for meditating on the past, and the drone of our scouting aeroplane, echoing curiously in the vault, set us clutching at the ropes again and calling to those above to haul us out.

Since the Senusites had been broken by our attacks, there was not enough of the actual living world remaining in our life on the desert to keep most of us interested or properly occupied. Our existence was both trying and monotonous, and most of us tried one method or another of getting transferred elsewhere. One way was to apply for a commission; another was to seek a transfer to the Air Force; but as the occupations of all in the Armoured Car Squadron were somewhat in the nature of skilled work the men could not be quickly replaced, and although transferring was not officially forbidden, in practice it was discouraged.

On 14th July I was at last given three days' leave in Alexandria. Three of us were to go together, and we mounted the Ford tender on duty in high spirits to drive down to the quay. The ship on which we were to travel was my old friend the Borulas, but the memories which the sight of her brought back to me were softened by time and the happiness of the present occasion. We set sail in the afternoon, and by the time darkness descended the sky had become overcast and a mist was rising.

A blind man could have seen that we three were on leave, and the Greek steward probably knew within a piastre or two how much money each of us carried in his pocket. He suggested in his oiliest tones, 'You lika veree nice deenna?' We considered this, making elaborate calculations which yielded no result in the British manner. He gave us a little rope until we were well in the slough of psycho-arithmetic and beginning to wobble; then he said comfortingly, in his most fatherly manner, 'Not costa much.' This pleasant assurance was like a firm rock under our feet, and we agreed expansively to partake of his veree nice deenna. We were already picturing to ourselves the rich and steaming dishes; and he added a fine, sweeping touch of colour to the picture when he said, 'All ri', you come seven o'glock in after saloon, I giva you plenty goot deenna.'

When seven strokes had been struck on the ship's bell we made our way to the after saloon, and at once our disillusioning began. The heat in the little cubby-hole was terrific, the stench of stale engine-oil was sickening, and the hammering and pounding of the ancient engines set the discoloured cutlery and the chipped salt-cellars on the table dancing like marionettes. It was with the greatest difficulty that we managed to convey to our mouths a little of the greasy water which our Greek magician announced to us as 'soop, veree nice,' for, to add to our difficulties, a wind had sprung up and the ship was beginning to roll. The only other dish that I remember was an unpleasant-looking mass of white tubes coiled on a plate, with a splash of something red in the middle. This was served with the remark, 'Macaronee, sauce tomatum: veree goot.' We talked cheerfully, so as to keep up the holiday atmosphere which was showing a tendency to vanish, but I was feeling anything but cheerful, and the faces of the other two were strained with the attempt to look on the bright side of things.

All the time the motion of the ship grew more violent, and at last I felt so ill that I was obliged to leave the table and lie down on one of the wooden benches that ran round the walls of the saloon. But here the vibration caused by the engines jerked my head up and down with maddening persistence. As I lay wondering what to do next a feeling came over me that if I could get up on deck in the fresh air I should be all right at once. I got up and staggered out of the door, grasped the rail of the companion-way, and crawled up the stairs. As I stepped out on the sea-washed deck, where all was black darkness, something hit me on the head, and I remembered nothing more until I heard a faint voice repeating my name. My two comrades were bending over me and we were in a cabin. Piecing together scraps of evidence after wards, I decided that I must have fainted as I stepped out and slid across the deck, being prevented from going overboard only by the fact that my legs passed one on either side of an iron stanchion supporting the rails.

The next morning we steamed into Matruh harbour over a sea as smooth as a mill-pond, and I felt entirely restored. On the following day at dawn we entered the busy harbour of Alexandria, and felt ourselves to be back in the great world once more.

It was a delightful experience to sit on chairs outside the cafes in the Rue Ramleh, sipping iced drinks, and feeling intensely civilized and cosmopolitan. The Western desert seemed like another world, and it hardly seemed possible that we could have got into this brave new world so easily. The Australians sitting at neighbouring tables, while agreeing with us that Alexandria was a place where a man could stretch his legs and get rid of the desert cramp, said it was not a patch on Sydney; but we did not believe that anything could be better than this. We went here and there, shopping, and doing errands for our friends at Sollum, such as getting buckles fitted to ancient wrist-watch straps, flints fitted to obsolete cigarette-lighters, or repairs done to the hinges of cheap cigarette-cases. There was something rich and strange in almost everything we saw in the varied shops, the tram-cars, the private motor cars, the men in civilian clothes, and especially the women in dainty hats and frocks. Even the blue sunlit sea hardly reminded us of the Bay of Sollum, for here it was sprinkled with pleasure boats and bathers.

Our leave came to an end and we returned, broke. On board the Borulas the Greek steward did not even ask us if we would like so much as a veree nice cup of coffee. If on the outward journey he could have told our wealth within a couple of piastres, he knew it exactly now. We threw down our blankets in the most sheltered spot we could find on deck, and began to solicit cups of cocoa from the scoundrel, on promise of future payment at Sollum.

The motion of the Borulas was gentle that night, and we sang songs together as we lay under our blankets beneath the stars. She did not put in at Matruh, and the next morning at about nine o'clock the mountains behind Sollum came in sight. Soon we were surrounded by a crowd of our comrades who had come down to the quay to find out whether we had done their various commissions, and back in the fort the tale of our mild adventures was quite an important event in the normal monotony of life.

Chapter Seven
The Expedition To Wadi Saal

The day after my return from leave some Italians from Bardia, to the north-west, paid us a visit. Distant dust clouds in the desert announced their approach, and soon we could hear the roar of their Fiat cars. They descended among us, dressed in smart grey-blue uniforms and with drooping plumes in their hats. We had hurriedly spread a meal for them of bully beef, bread, and beer, to be followed by tinned pineapple, the last two items being purchased in the canteen with the proceeds of a whip-round in the Battery. We thought our hospitality would seem rather poor to them, but apparently they found all in order, for they stayed to tea and supper as well. We got on very well with them, although our only means of communication was scraps of French, and one of them, Vittorio Emanuel by name, told funny stories which were very good indeed. He told them in Italian, and what they were about I never learnt, but his manner of telling them was certainly comic, and as he somehow made it perfectly plain when we were all supposed to roar out great bursts of laughter, the proceedings went off with great hilarity. Others performed card-tricks or sang songs; one with a fine tenor voice singing O Sole Mio, in which we were all able to join to some extent.

Another object of our visitors was to make plans with us for carrying on the war. Their spies, or agents as we call them when they belong to our own side, had brought them information to the effect that thousands of the Senusites, with Nuri Bey at their head, were concealed in a camp in the Wadi Saal, a deep cleft running down to the sea, between Bardia and Tabrouk. The plan finally decided on was that two batteries of our armoured cars, a company of the Australian Camel Corps, and the Italians in their Fiats, should set out from Sollum together at sunset on 25th July and proceed along the Tabrouk road. At a point some miles this side of the Wadi Saal one battery would turn off to the right and make for the right bank of the Wadi. The company of Camel Corps and the Italians were to continue along the road with the other battery until they came to the Wadi Sarat, which was an upper reach of the Saal. Here they, too, were to turn right-handed and advance down the Wadi itself; while the second armoured car battery was to go some miles further before turning to the right and closing on the left bank of the Wadi. By this means it was hoped to kill or capture all the occupants of the enemy's camp, which would be completely surrounded - on the north by a monitor firing shells from the sea; on the east and west by an armoured car battery respectively; and on the south by the Australians and Italians. Fire was to be opened by all four attacking parties simultaneously at eleven o'clock on the morning of the 26th.

The column, a mile long, duly left Sollum as the sun disappeared, and proceeded in a north-westerly direction till dark, when we halted for the night. No fires were allowed, and after eating a little food in the darkness those who were not on guard duty lay down to sleep.

At three o'clock in the morning we were awakened by the sentries, and since it was uncertain when we should have another chance to eat, we opened tins of bully and made a hasty meal. Inside one of the cars a primus stove was employed to boil water for tea, and soon the welcome cup was ready.

At four o'clock we moved slowly forward in the dark for a further twenty-five miles, and then the order was given to the leading battery to put on speed and make its detour to the western bank of the Wadi. As the light increased I could see that the Italians looked different from what their appearance had been at Sollum. They had packed away all the smart uniforms and hats, and wore dirty, shapeless grey clothes. This gave us cause for wonder, for in our army we only had field-service kit, peace-time splendour being unheard of.

Soon the time came for us to turn off to the right, leaving the Italians and Australians to proceed on their way to the head of the Wadi. Once having left the road, we found the going terribly rough; great boulders had to be avoided at every few yards, and often we had to stop and remove large stones to one side before we could proceed on our way. There were so many delays that we presently began to fear that we should not be in position for the attack by the appointed time. Twice the base chamber of a car struck against a sharp rock, and in both instances a great deal of the lubricating oil escaped before the damage could be temporarily repaired.

As we crawled slowly forward we were suddenly cheered by the sight of the blue ocean, but we could see no sign of the monitor with our field-glasses, although it was already nearly eleven o'clock. Our excitement was growing more intense every minute, for we were now almost on the edge of the Wadi. It was a wide depression, filled with large stones which gave excellent cover to anyone who wished to conceal himself, and the steepness of its sides made a surprise attack difficult, if it was to be pushed home quickly.

After a brief halt to ensure that everything was ready, I looked at my watch and found that it was just eleven o'clock. We had only half a dozen yards to go in order to get to the edge of the Wadi. I lowered the armour lid in front, gave the word to the gunner to be ready with his gun and, peering through the slit, drove forward. The Wadi opened out beneath us, cut deep into the earth as though with a great knife, and down in the bottom there were scores of rough shacks and tents, amongst which a crowd of Arabs moved about or lolled on the ground. For a moment we were almost spellbound by the sight; then the stabbing spatter of the gun broke the hot silence. At once the whole of the Wadi bed was thrown into commotion, the men grabbing their rifles, and running this way and that, looking for vantage-points. Suddenly I shouted, 'Look ! There's Nuri!' The piebald horse, ready saddled, stood tethered outside a hut, and Nuri himself, the lower part of his face covered with lather, appeared to be shaving with the aid of a piece of mirror hung on the wall of the hut. It was his manner at the sound of our gun which convinced me that it must be him and no other. He looked round sharply in our direction and was perfectly still for a couple of seconds; then he made some rapid gestures, and was plainly issuing orders. This done, he slashed through the tethering rope of his horse with the razor which he held in his hand, sprang on her back, wheeled her round, and was gone down the Wadi like a streak of lightning.

We could see our other battery now, and soon its guns were rattling bullets into the depression from the opposite side. Suddenly a thunderous report came from seaward, and we knew that the monitor was at her station. A heavy shell burst in the middle of the Wadi, and was followed by others. The Senusites could be seen running down the Wadi towards the sea, but Nuri had vanished. The Italians had now come on the scene in their light Fiat cars, built and geared for mountain work. Coming into the Wadi from the inland side they were able, by the exercise of care, to drive right down it. When they reached the sea they guessed, by the direction being taken by the fugitives, that Nuri had turned towards the west and ridden along the beach. A signal was made to the monitor and a fast motor boat was launched by her to make a search, but without the desired result. Nuri had escaped us yet again.

Some of the Senusites maintained a spirited opposition after the Italian cars had passed their hiding places amongst the rocks, but before long all those who did not take to flight were shot or captured. It was impossible to pursue them in cars in such country, and those who fled got away unmolested. A Ford tender turned a complete somersault, but this was our only casualty.

The action being over we scrambled down to the camp, where we found gardens laid out between the huts and tents. Ammunition and other stores which had been landed from Turkish or German ships were stored in caves cut in the solid rock and fitted with strong wooden doors and great padlocks. The place was well chosen, for, everything being of the same yellowish colour as the Wadi itself, even aircraft were not likely to be attracted by the sight of anything unusual. The huts were very similar to boulders at a distance, and the tents were such as were used by the Bedouins.

The clearing up of this place was of some importance, for it was plain that it had been the chief place for the importation of arms and supplies. The prisoners were handed over to the Italians, who intended to take them back to Bardia, and there to squeeze information out of them. The Italian commander also invited us, his British allies, to spend the night in that hospitable fort.

It was nearly dark when we all assembled again on the Tabrouk road, and as conquering heroes we switched on our lights at full power, in defiance of all laws, whether of the desert or of Whitehall. The powerful beams lit up the rocks for a mile ahead, and occasionally showed flitting gazelles or the gleaming eyes of a jackal. We made the best speed we could, and at last the beacon light at Bardia blinked its welcome at us.

That night we sat up late, while corks popped merrily and the ration wine of our hosts flowed freely. Bowls of steaming spaghetti were placed on the table and liberal helpings served out to us, so that our belts had to be loosened as well as our tongues. We drank the health of Italy and the Italians in many a bumper, and they returned the compliment. Vittorio Emanuel told me in his French what a high regard he and his people had for me and mine, and I told him in my French what a high regard I and mine had for him and his, and we grew more and more friendly as the night went on. First he sang a song, and then I told a story; and while he was singing his song and I was telling my story most of our gallant comrades were similarly occupied. The babel of English, Italian and French grew louder and foggier, the grimacing and the chaos of gesticulation grew more and more earnest, and more and more uniform. It was a tipple alliance, which gradually merged in slumber.

In the morning I found myself under my blanket in the open, so I suppose we finished our session under the stars.

Chapter Eight
Patrolling The Desert

After the affair at the Wadi Saal we spent our time in monotonous routine duties at the fort of Sollum, varied by occasional patrols in the desert. The enemy were believed to have withdrawn far to the southward, and our expeditions were extended in that direction for the most part. We now spent a good deal of time in training carrier pigeons, at first taking them out ten miles before releasing them, then twenty miles, then thirty or forty, and so on, gradually increasing the distance until we were able to send messages to Sollum from distances of over a hundred miles.

Another of our tasks was to fill in details on the almost blank maps of the country, and occasionally we would run out fifty or sixty miles in order to drop intelligence agents at convenient points from which they could make their way to the enemy's camps.

Our greatest luxury was a swim in the sea, and the moment we reached Sollum after a long run in the desert there was a general rush for the bathing-place. Down the mountain road we drove in a tender, kicking off boots, shirts and shorts as we went; and then, arrived on the beach, we sprang down, and with a whoop of joy took to the water like a flock of ducks. After days spent in the blazing desert the mere sight of the clear blue sea was like a foretaste of Paradise.

Once a grand concert was organized, in honour of a visit by the General, and a comic sketch was staged, complete with appropriate scenery. It was made more amusing than the author had intended by the awkward army boots of the actresses, and the fact that their bosoms kept on slipping down too low. Another turn was given by a Cockney poet, who recited a masterpiece of his own, beginning:

On the road to Sollum Bay
Fleas and lizards bask all day.

In spite of loud protests and cries of 'Lie down, Shakespeare!' the poet went on and on without a pause, with out expression, and without hurry, like a very regular sergeant reading orders to the guard. But we had no intention of putting up with that, and the chorus, 'Sit down! Sit down!' roared by a hundred throats to the tune of Big Ben's chimes, at last caused the poet to fade away.

On 30th August two of our spies came in with information that the Senusites were making their chief base in the Jaghbub Oasis, nearly two hundred miles from the coast, and that their supply caravans to that place were passing through Bir Hakim, the place where the Tara prisoners had been kept. This was important news, and it behoved us to harry their communications without delay.

At dawn on the 31st we started out towards Bir Wair, and after going about thirty miles in a westerly direction we turned to the south and made for Bir El Shekka, a junction of caravan roads, about a hundred miles from Sollum. This place was about sixty miles from the road which connected Bir Hakim with Jaghbub. We reached Shekka half an hour before noon, and there a halt was called, tarpaulins were rigged between the tops of every two cars as a protection from the fierce rays of the sun, and under these we ate our midday meal and rested. When the sun had lost some of its power we rose and prepared to reconnoitre the distant road, with the hope of holding up an enemy caravan. With the armoured cars in front and the transport tenders in the rear, we moved off in a south-westerly direction. The going was good and the pace swift, and soon we came to the track we were seeking - a number of narrow tracings in the sandy soil, little wider than sheep tracks, and, though winding about this way and that, keeping steadily in one general direction and roughly parallel to one another. This was an ancient desert highway, marked out by the camels of a thousand years. We concealed all the cars behind rising ground close beside it, dismounted some of the guns and placed them on tripods in convenient positions, arranged ammunition boxes in handy places beside them, and then waited.

The sun was sinking towards the west and I had begun to fear that we should have to spend the night on watch, when suddenly one of the gunners said, 'Look! What's that?' We all strained our eyes in the direction of his pointing finger and saw faint wisps of dust on the horizon. Gradually we could make out a train of swinging camels, which appeared to be heavily laden. This seemed likely to be the quarry which we were seeking.

We waited in silence and allowed the leader to get almost abreast of us before making a sign. Then one of our guns crashed out, sending a stream of bullets harmlessly across his front. The effect of this greeting was instantaneous, but not exactly what their leader desired. All the camel-drivers unslung their rifles from their shoulders and began firing them at random, apparently making no attempt to aim at anything; but the chief leapt to the ground and ran down the line, shouting and gesticulating to the others as he went. It was plain that he wanted to stop their antics so that he could deal with the awkward situation through diplomatic channels. His policy was to be one of bluff, and as soon as the firing had ceased they all fell in train for their parts, like well-trained actors. An expression of calm unconsciousness settled on their swarthy faces: their hostile glances changed to a sort of polite inquiry; and there was now nothing to distinguish them outwardly from a peaceable trading caravan out on a hard day's march for the purpose of earning an honest crust by the sweat of their brows.

We had now stood up and shown ourselves, and the chief advanced towards our position, throwing open his cloak as he came so as to show that he was unarmed, helpless, innocent, and good. Mohammed, our chief spy, philosopher and guide, went to meet him, and there began a violent argument between these two old friends, for Mohammed, having been purified by British gold from his gun-running in the Senusite interest, was now more zealous in the Allied cause than we were. The dispute, enlivened by whirling, smacking and thumping gesticulation, grew hotter and hotter, until at last the noble Mohammed spat very expressively on the ground his sense of disgust at the other's double-dealing, pushed roughly past him and, drawing his long knife from its sheath, slashed through the girths of one of the camels, allowing its load to slip to the ground. The chief appealed to us with outstretched hands and suffering eyes against this unseemly violence, and appeared to swear by Allah that he was white all through. 'Kizb!' yelled Mohammed, who was plainly determined even at the cost of his life that the truth should prevail. 'A lie! Shuf! Look!' and his knife was on the point of slitting a sack. But the chief could not bear to be called a liar. and, before the other's knife could touch the sack, he had sprung on him. At this all the followers of that good chief groaned and opened fire with their rifles from behind their camels. Instantly the rattle of our machine-guns rent the air, and several score of camels fell dead or wounded. The Arabs ceased fire, and we rushed to separate the two old friends who were still struggling together.

Then we began the work of slashing open the sacks and bales of merchandise, an occupation which we had to do as quickly as possible, for the sun had set and darkness was about to close down. All the sacks contained a nourishing mixture of corn and cartridges, all that was necessary to sustain the

Senusites on active service.

We camped on the scene of the action, and a very unpleasant night followed. I hardly slept at all, for the ceaseless moaning of the wounded camels was terrible. As soon as dawn began to come into the sky we got up and shot every camel which yet remained alive, and when we left they were lying along the track as a warning to others whom it might concern. There were one hundred and thirty of them.

I do not know whether it was in consequence of an accusation made by the chief or what, but something gave rise to a suspicion about the whiteness of Mohammed's heart, and after he had been interrogated through the interpreter it was thought desirable to search him. Some of the dirty scraps of paper which were found in the nooks and crannies of his rags appeared to give proof that he was not entirely converted to the Allied cause, but that he was still using his own judgment about which side he should support at any particular moment. He was asked to consider himself under arrest, but the effect of this British panacea made him splutter more than ever with outraged verbosity. He was therefore informed that anything he might say would be taken down and used in evidence against him. I don't know who was to take it down, as, unless Esmi knew some form of shorthand in which a whole paragraph could be represented by a sign the size of a dot, I am afraid he could not have kept pace with Mohammed's furious unburdening of his mind. Not that this was of any importance. It was laid down in some statute that the prisoner was to be warned. This had now been done; our legal position was unassailable; all was in order; and Mohammed having got into my car, just before noon the column set out on its return to Sollum.

The going was fairly good, and we made rapid progress, but the heat of the sun seemed worse than ever. For mile after mile I drove on steadily, with my eyes fixed on the ground in front, for I was leading the column and had to choose the best way through every patch of rocks or sand which we encountered. It was past mid-afternoon when suddenly Mohammed, who was sitting at the back of the car, shouted, 'Stanna!' I was only too thankful for the chance of a brief rest and I quickly brought her to a standstill. 'What's the matter now?' I asked. He was standing up and pointing forward, pouring out a spate of Arabic. I grabbed my glasses and looked through them in the direction he was pointing to. Presently I could distinguish camel riders in the haze. On driving up to them we found that they were a detachment of our own camel corps on patrol. They had been bound for the place which we had just left, but on hearing our news they changed their direction.

On reaching Bir Shekka we made our camp for the night. The well at this place was a deep pit in the rock, with a small puddle of dirty water in the bottom of it. So it appeared at first sight, but on climbing down into the bottom a dark hole was seen in the rock face, so situated as to be invisible from above. Crawling on hands and knees through this hole the traveller came into a natural tunnel, and after making his way along its slimy floor for some distance he arrived at a running spring of cool clear water. It was not without trouble that we managed to fill our fantassis, but it was well worth all our exertions to get a supply of such pure sweet water. Water is the staff of life in the desert, and its quality varies so much that half a pint of good water there is a gift of more value than a dozen quarts of the best champagne in Europe.

At dawn we struck camp and went on over undulating country of alternate sand and rock. In some of the depressions we drove on to what looked like firm ground, but suddenly found our wheels dropping through the thin surface into red mud. Then it was necessary to change without an instant's delay into low gear, often from top to bottom in a single slam, so as to force a way through the quagmire. As we came in sight of

Sollum, the fort, glittering above the ground haze, looked as though it was suspended in the air.

They already had our news of the capture of the caravan, for Herbert, one of our pigeons, had duly arrived with a note from the Jaghbub road.

The period of duty at Sollum for my battery had now come to an end, and on 5th September we set out on the journey of one hundred and forty-five miles to Matruh, covering the distance in five hours of continuous running. Thousands of Arabs were encamped outside the entrenchments, where they were given rations of food, for the blockade of the coast and the Egyptian frontier had caused starvation of a kind that even Arabs could not endure. This is a well-known way of taming lions and other wild creatures - starve them thoroughly first and then offer them a dole of food, so that they feed out of your hand, or not at all.

Matruh was a pleasant enough station. The country round about it was flat, and billows of silver sand rolled away in front of the stone huts for three hundred yards to the little harbour and the blue sea. The harbour was very shallow, and dredgers were continually at work deepening it, but only small coasting streamers could ever get inside. Even these often got stranded on the harmless sandy bottom. Beyond it to the west there was a shallow lagoon, beside which lay the village with its mosque, amongst palm groves and other vegetation. On a rock before the harbour entrance stood the lighthouse and a small fort manned by coastguards.

Our days were now chiefly spent in repairing the cars and other equipment, and in getting ready for our forthcoming trek across the desert to the great oases of the south, which belonged to Egypt, but which had been occupied by the Senusites under Ahmad, while Jaafar and Nuri were making their efforts to advance on Alexandria. In the evenings we attended lectures intended to make us familiar with the very rough maps of the country, which were all that existed; but these harangues were not very helpful, as the lecturers had never been to the places they tried to describe, any more than we had. We should have to work largely by rule-of-thumb, as we had done hitherto.

In our spare time we gathered water-melons and wild tomatoes, or shot quail; and one of our chief 'sports' was to watch a scorpion and a centipede fight a duel in a glass jar. The centipede would manoeuvre so as to avoid the sting on the end of its adversary's tail, which it brings over its back so as to stab an object in front of it, and at the first opportunity it would whip itself round the scorpion's body like a snake, taking only one turn at first. The position it chose was always such that it could not be reached by the stabbing tail. Presently the centipede would take a second turn about the scorpion's body, and then a third; and all the while its opponent would grow more and more violent and infuriated. Not trying to inflict any wound itself, the centipede would draw its folds tighter and tighter, like a python, while it seemed to wait for something to happen. At last the scorpion would begin to show signs of weakness, and then the centipede's stranglehold would appear to grow yet tighter, until the scorpion with a last effort would drive its sting into its own back near the head, either through inability to control its actions properly or with the deliberate intention of committing hara kiri. In a few moments more it would roll over helpless, with the victorious centipede still wound about it.

On 15th September the thermometer registered 115° in the shade, and the motionless air was stifling. I was stricken with fever, could not sleep, and became delirious; but somebody gave me opium, so that I fell into a doze. The next day, however, I lapsed into complete unconsciousness, and when I came to I found myself in the hospital. Feverish days of delirium followed, but at last the medical officer accepted my statement that all was again well with me, and declared me fit for duty. I was overjoyed to get away from the boredom of life in hospital, and I hurried as fast as I could to rejoin my friends in the stone huts. My battery had just returned to Sollum for another spell of outpost duty, and instructions had been left that I was to follow with 'Blast' as soon as I was discharged from hospital. Accompanied by the Repair Staff-Sergeant, I ran the car out for a test, and knowing her so well I was able to detect the need of several adjustments which had been made necessary by the overhaul which she had undergone during my absence. On the following morning at seven o'clock I started out for Sollum, with the sergeant and corporal of the Battery as passengers.

We had agreed that as nobody was dependent on us in any way we would make a fast run, and now with the open desert in front of us and nothing but our dust streaming out behind, I let her have her head. The speedometer showed nearly seventy miles an hour at times, which was not bad, for she was carrying three men with all their kit and three tons of armour. After an hour or so we stopped to eat our breakfast of bully, bread, and tea. At half-past nine we came in sight of Sidi Barrani; seventy-five miles in two and a half hours, including a halt of over half an hour, was a record for this stretch of road, and we wrote a note of it inside the car as a support for our future bragging.

At Sidi Barrani we slipped into the sea for a quick bathe, and then away again on the open road, thanking the gods for these moments of freedom. I sometimes envied the desert scallywags for the freedom of their existence; in Europe we know nothing like it.

At Bakbak we already had the mountains rising on our left hand, while on the right the glittering foam of the sea waves almost washed our wheels in places. Soon we saw the Abbas fort, perched above the ornamental terraces which we had made, and with the Union Jack floating from its mast. We roared on through the lines of horses and mules, and the groups of men who cheered or shouted at us as we passed. Our arrival was an event to them, for stagnation and the drill book now filled their days.

Back in our fort at the top of the cliff we found that things had changed for the worse there also. Getting up in the morning after stretching like a cat for five or ten minutes was no longer allowed; all had to be on parade and dressed by the right half a minute after reveille had sounded. Soldiers should love their sergeant-major, but since our former sergeant had attained that exalted rank it must be confessed that he had forfeited some of our regard. He had degenerated into a martinet, and was often a bad-tempered one. To do him justice, he certainly gave us some warning of what to expect from day to day. When we saw that his nose was blue we felt comforted, for that meant that he intended to be reasonable and sweet; when his nose was purple we knew he would be a little wayward; but, by jingo, when it was red we had to prepare for squalls and thunderstorms, which no amount of keeping open the weather eye would help us to escape. You cannot serve two masters, and I suppose that it was unavoidable that the higher our sergeant-major rose in the esteem of his superior officers the lower he was bound to fall in ours. No anatomists ever studied a nose as closely as we studied his.

Chapter Nine
Wadi Zawia

One afternoon a Bedouin belonging to a friendly tribe came in with the information that a band of Senusites were hiding in a cleft in the rocky coast towards Tabrouk. The place, which he described in detail, was called Wadi Zawia. When agreement had been reached concerning the amount of his reward, and not before, he promised to lead us to the enemy camp; and at sunset on 27th October four armoured cars with their transport moved out to westward, and took the now familiar road towards Tripoli. Esmi and the Bedouin sat in the rear part of my car, and as I was the last of the column on this day, and was thus relieved of the responsibility of choosing the route and setting the pace, and could trail along free of care behind the others, I was able to profit by the conversation of my passengers. Esmi announced that the Bedouin's name was Mahmud, that he was second in command of his tribe, that he had three wives and many children. This all seemed very respectable; but there was an unpleasant innuendo in the next bit of information which was passed on to me, to the effect that Mahmud's chief had only to die for that noble Arab to come into his full power. The idea was probably Esmi's, but it was quite a natural view of the matter, for when he had interpreted it to Mahmud the noble informer nodded his head at me and stroked his beard with great dignity, and appeared to be considering what date he should choose for taking upon himself the supreme power. As we were operating within the Italian sphere we had an Italian officer with us, as had now become the custom; and at his suggestion we made our first night's camp at a place about thirty miles from Sollum, drawing the cars up in a circle with guns pointing out. After eating a meal we lay down to sleep, but at one o'clock in the morning I was awakened to do my turn on guard. I pulled on my greatcoat, for the night was chilly and wet with dew, and shouldering my rifle began tramping round the circle of cars and sleeping men. Moving clouds frequently obscured the moon, and the silence was broken by snores and an occasional jackal howl. Presently I thought I heard something moving, and I gripped my rifle in both hands, but I could see nothing in the direction from which the sound had come. Then all at once I saw two shining eyes staring at me out of the blackness. I stood as though petrified. The eyes moved: suddenly I yelled, 'Guard! Turn out!' and covered the thing with my rifle. Everybody now scrambled out of his blanket and grabbed his rifle. 'Look!' I cried, as some of them ran up to me; and they, too, stood speechless, nobody doing anything. Then the gleaming eyes disappeared. Some of the men rushed forward, and I was on the point of firing my rifle as a relief to my feelings when the night was filled with shrieks of laughter. They had found that our midnight visitor was a stray donkey. This was remembered against me for some time.

Before dawn tea was hurriedly prepared, and then the Ford tenders were hitched on to the armoured cars to be towed round in circles, for this was the only means by which they could be started on damp mornings. When the engines were all turning satisfactorily we drove away to the north-west. Soon the ground became very uneven and stony, and our speed was reduced to a crawl. The place into which we had come looked like a graveyard, with tombstones slanting at all sorts of angles. Five miles from our objective a halt was called, and each armoured car was detailed to its station. It was impossible to carry out our original plan of rushing the camp from this point, as the ground was too rough for the cars, so we dismounted some of the guns and went forward on foot. From the edge of the Wadi an uneven slope descended to a wide, sandy depression, across which streams of water flowed from the rocks above, winding their way to the sea. At the inland side of this place stood a number of wooden huts, surrounded by terraced fields and gardens, and approached by winding pathways. At first we saw several figures of men walking amongst these dwellings, but in a moment they caught sight of us above them, and like a flash they were off across the sand flat and the dunes beyond. Only an aeroplane could have followed them. We crawled down to the huts as quickly as we could, with rifles and revolvers in our hands, and proceeded to ransack every one of them, bringing all the contents into the open. Having taken everything which might be of use to us, we poured petrol on the rest, including the huts themselves. Then our captain advanced to set fire to the piles. The flames quickly gathered power, and in a moment there was a terrific explosion which threw the officer violently to the ground. We lifted him up and got him back to the cars somehow, and then set off on our slow return to Sollum, where he went into hospital.

On examining my car I found that a cross member of her frame was broken, and she was laid up until a new one had arrived from Matruh and been fitted - a difficult job, as we had few tools for such work.

The winter had now come in earnest, and on 1st November a violent storm struck our camp in a welter of thunder and lightning and masses of rain. The water rushed in torrents over the edge of the plateau and down the mountain slopes. Our fine new road from the plain was almost entirely washed away by the roaring cascades, and the infantry camp below was completely inundated, causing a wild scramble by the troops to save their gear from being swept into the sea.

Screaming sandstorms also swept across the Libyan desert with frightful velocity, piling deep drifts against all obstructions. One day in the course of our exercises on foot we marched out in the direction of Bir Wair, following an old car track which showed faintly in the surface of the plain. Presently a sand-devil made its appearance, careering towards us at a great pace. The nearer it came the larger it grew, and everything movable which lay in its path was snatched up and whirled sky high. Bending this way and that, like a snake standing on its head, it passed howling close to us on a zigzag course, went over the edge of the plateau and so out to sea. Immediately after it had gone a sandstorm descended upon us, and we groped for the car-track which we had been following so as to return by the way we had come, but it had already disappeared. We staggered through the stinging storm, making our way back to the fort as directly as we could without anything to guide us; but after a time we were cheered by the sound of a gun being fired at intervals as a signal to us.

On 19th November a new intelligence agent joined us, Ali by name, but soon known to the troops as Ali Smuggler, for his profession in civil life was the importing of opium and other dope into the country without any legal formalities. All our 'agents' were low characters from the mingled fringes of East and West, for, in their natural state, the Arabs look upon spying as a dirty trade, especially spying on their own race in the interests of aliens. We used to find much entertainment in watching Ali Smuggler tell his mean tales with the air of a hero justly proud of honourable exploits, helped by a word or two now and then from Esmi the interpreter. The old rascal's long, bony claws waved and grabbed in the air as he spoke fiercely of his methods of tipping unwanted confederates out of boats, or ham stringing the camels of those who might pursue him. We gathered, with the help of Esmi, that he knew every creek and wadi along the coast from Beyrout to Algiers, and that he could dodge any coastguard system ever invented, landing his contraband dope at night in a small boat from a ship out of sight of land. When he and his faithful comrades had carried the stuff into their secret cave a fight would usually ensue before it was finally shared out; after which those fit to travel would make their way across the desert and enter Egypt by unfrequented ways - and so to Cairo and the other towns of the Delta, where dope-taking was so popular that little boys used to sing the Cocaine Song and the Hashish Song in the streets, sniffing up pinches of flour and smoking fag-ends in decayed pipes between the verses. We wanted to know what happened when he was stopped by the police; and at the sound of the word his old wrinkled face looked as fierce as a tiger's, he spat venomously on the ground, and out of his mouth rushed a torrent of hissing, snarling speech. The little interpreter said to us mildly that this good intelligence agent had always resented hotly any interference offered to him in the earning of his living. Those were infidels who dared to hinder a free man in his journeyings to and fro. Outraged innocence and indignation were perfectly expressed in the old man's face as he denounced those lawless men. But when he proceeded to speak of receiving payment for the stuff - £20, £30, for a little bit which you could hold in your hand - then his voice grew almost gentle, and his wicked old eyes beamed love and goodwill to all men. But things were not what they had been. Why, at one time he thought nothing of owning £500 in gold, or of paying £20 or £30 for a camel. He needed a fast camel in his profession, for the coastguards (Allah curse their fathers!) had very fast camels, only they did not know how to ride them.

I inquired what his plans were for the future, and he made gestures in reply, throwing out his hands, shrugging his shoulders, and clapping the palm of his hand to his forehead, as though in despair of being able to find a field for his talents. Esmi said he was prepared to join any tough gang who would offer him good prospects. I said, 'Well, he has joined us.' When this had been translated to the old man he roared out a flood of old, rasping laughter for the first time.

Chapter Ten
A Trip To Alexandria

We now had to keep some sort of watch from the north on the Senusite headquarters in the Siwa Oasis, as the Egyptian garrison was doing from the east. The distance from the coast was over one hundred and fifty miles in a straight line, and it was highly necessary that we should survey and mark the most direct routes, if possible with water-holes on them at convenient intervals. The maps in our possession were almost blank, and even the information which they did contain was often unreliable. In any case, the ground had never yet been surveyed for motor cars, and we had to mark the best routes with stone cairns which could be seen from a great distance, standing out above the mirage like dark beacons.

On one of these expeditions we took rations for seven days, and loaded the Ford tenders with full fantassis. There were four armoured cars with a lieutenant in command, and we were accompanied by a major and some men of the Royal Engineers. We first made our way to the south-east, along the edge of the plateau, picking our route cautiously amongst the stones, while the sun rose out of the east and glinted on the sea below. At the end of the day we came to a track which led from Bakbak to Siwa, and here we pitched our camp. From this point two of the armoured cars were to make an extended reconnaissance to the southward, taking with them the R.E. major and his men, and half the transport vehicles. My car was one of the two to be left at the advanced base. Early the next morning we watched the expedition disappear in wisps of dust over the horizon, and then turned to and made ourselves a comfortable bivouac where we could while away the days until the others returned. Close at hand I found a curious well with four tunnel-like entrances. At the inner end of these tunnels a spring of clear water flowed, though, glancing at the place from the outside, no one would have dreamed such a thing existed there.

The place in which we were encamped was a dead level, almost without a stone on it, and nothing broke the low horizon all around us, not even a cairn. There was no sign of life anywhere outside our little camp, no beast, no bird, and the loneliness was complete. Three nights we had passed in this solitude, when on the fourth day at noon a wisp of dust appeared on the southern skyline, at the edge of our world. Soon we could see with glasses that it was indeed our comrades returning; the leading car could be seen rising and dipping with the undulations of the ground, now out of sight, now in full view on top of a rise. We made our fire send up a great smoke to guide them to our camp in case they had not seen us, and soon we heard the roar of their open exhausts. As they pulled up we hastened to inquire their news, and it was plain by their begrimed appearance and bloodshot eyes that they had had a grim journey. They had got within thirty miles of Siwa, putting up cairns and noting the position of wells.

When they had eaten a meal we all moved away towards the north at an easy pace, as we intended to go back by Bakbak and the coast road, getting home on the following day. At sundown we camped again in the open desert, and on the following morning drove the cars with some difficulty down a cliff to the coastal plain. Here we had good going again nearly all the way to the road, on reaching which we turned westward and reached Sollum in the evening. It was good to see the twinkling lights of the camp again after spending a whole week in the empty desert, and it was even better to hear the Cockney voices calling, 'What cheer, matey!' as we passed through.

Soon after this expedition our General paid a visit to the

Italians at Bardia, and a day or two after his return nearly all the troops in Sollum began to pack their gear for a move. They soon departed to the east, and we were left as an outpost. But worse than this was to follow, for we now heard that we were to move our camp far out into the desert, where even sea-bathing would be denied to us. One of our cars had to be returned to Alexandria, and I was fortunate enough to be given the job of driving it there. On the appointed morning, having previously taken the precaution of drawing some of my overdue pay, I set out at eight o'clock, with a corporal as passenger. I took the car along at an easy pace, for being dressed in a clean drill tunic and well-ironed shorts, which I had paid the captain's servant to wash and press for me, I had no intention of courting any unnecessary repair work. We were both in high spirits as we skimmed along, and hummed tunes in chorus. But presently a black object came in sight on the road ahead, and as we drew nearer we saw that it was a Ford car, evidently disabled, which had been left there by somebody in our Brigade. I intended to drive past it and straight on to Matruh, but my friend the corporal said, 'Let's tow it into Sidi Barrani.' In this untimely suggestion he persisted, so out came our tow-rope and he hitched it on and then took the wheel of the Ford.

Before starting I warned him that I intended to put on speed to make up for the time we had lost, and we were soon shooting along at a great rate, throwing up a huge cloud of dust. We reached Sidi Barrani at half-past eleven, and there I pulled up and jumped out. But I could not see my friend the corporal. The Ford was there, but where was he? Yes, he was there too, but in colour he was indistinguishable from the car, both being thickly coated with light brown dust. After a little recrimination between us he ran down to the sea to bathe, and presently returned in his shirt and carrying his drill suit in his hand. I helped him to brush the dust off his clothes, and then we left with as little delay as possible for the next stage.

The next forty miles of road was level, and so straight that its furthest visible point lay directly ahead on the horizon. The Rolls Royce sped along swiftly with open exhaust, like a torpedo shooting between the dunes. Soon I was amongst familiar landmarks, and we came to soft sand which demanded a slower speed. At last we came to the top of a low ridge and saw sleepy Matruh white against the blue background of the Mediterranean. Here too we found that the garrison had been reduced to a mere handful, who eked out a lonely existence and complained of the monotony of life. We spent the night here, as the next stage to the railhead at Dabaa was a long one, and the way unknown to us. The captain in command at Matruh showed a fatherly desire to advise us about the difficulties of the road, and we were glad to have his warnings and details of the bad patches.

The next morning we started after sunrise and found the road in excellent condition for the first thirty-five miles. After this, however, the going became more difficult as we encountered patches of soft sand. I was driving carelessly with one hand while looking at the view and talking to the corporal, when suddenly the wheel seemed to fly out of my grasp and the car lurched and floundered in loose sand. Our speed, which had been thirty miles an hour, was checked so violently that I was thrown forward against the wheel. She was in top gear, but making a quick double-clutch I raced the engine and brought her straight down to second, missing third. She went on grinding grimly through the sand, and I thought she was going to get through it; but no, she gradually slowed. I slipped her into bottom gear and the engine began to squeal as it flew round with the driving shaft. I worked the steering wheel madly this way and that, trying to find an easier way where there was none, but it was of no use. She crawled on a little further, and then stuck fast with her axles buried deep in the sand - nearly four tons of dead metal.

We looked at each other without speaking. On other similar occasions we had had scores of hands to push behind and pull on ropes tied to the axle, but now we were helpless. Two men could do nothing with four tons of iron and steel, and we were miles and miles from the nearest human beings. Suddenly I shouted, 'Come on! We must get out of this somehow,' and jumped out on the sand. Had she kept going for another ten yards we should have been on firm ground again, but for two hundred yards she had ploughed a deep track in the desert, and she could do no more. The corporal was a gunner and had no suggestions to offer in this emergency. I told him to go and gather as much solid material as he could find – scrub bushes and stones – and then I took the shovel from the car and began to dig away the sand from under the front axle. The corporal came back with his arms full of stones, and telling him to go and get some more I began to hammer those he had brought under the axle so as to make a foundation for the jack. But as I worked the jack lever I saw that the car did not come up at all; my exertions merely caused the stones to sink deep in the sand. I pressed the release lever, put more stones under the jack and began again; but still the weight of the car forced the stones down uselessly. The corporal continued to bring me stones, and both of us grumbled continually at the turn affairs had taken. We both had flung off most of our carefully laundered clothes and the delights of Alexandria seemed very far away. At last I felt I had had enough of driving stones into a bottomless quicksand, and we settled down to make tea and change the subject for a while. Suddenly the corporal said, 'Aren't those buildings out there?' I looked where he was pointing and saw what appeared to be several ruined houses. It was one of the landmarks we had been told of, called Seven Houses.

This find seemed to offer chances of getting better material for our purpose, for the stones which the corporal had been able to find had been too small to be of much use. As soon as we had finished our tea we hastened towards Seven Houses, and when we got there the corporal cried, 'Here you are! Just the thing!' I hurried up to see what he had found, and saw at his feet a circular millstone, weighing half a ton. I said yes, that was just the thing, and told him to take it back to the car. He looked hurt at this. But we found wooden beams in the buildings, and each carrying one of them we returned hopefully whence we had come. We found the two lengths of timber were too long to go between the front and rear wheels, so it still remained necessary to jack the front axle up clear of the sand. The corporal went and collected more and more stones, and at last I managed to get it up into the required position. We pushed one end of the timber as far under the rear wheel as it would go, and then forced it down under the front wheel. Having done this on both sides we laid a thick mat of brushwood in front of the car as far as the firm ground, first clearing away the worst of the loose sand. Then I got into the car, tightened the sling so that it would keep me closer to the wheel, and started the engine. I slipped in the first gear, and with a violent squeal she lurched forward. She came to the end of the timber track and there seemed to drop with a great jerk, but she went on, and in a few moments I had pulled her up on firm ground.

The sun was sinking low as we started off smoothly for Dabaa. Shooting past the Seven Houses, we roared along at high speed, but keeping a very sharp look-out for further obstacles. It was almost dark when we caught sight of the twinkling lights of the railway terminus.

At Dabaa we had to put the car on a truck as the rest of the journey was to be done by rail, and on arrival we were told by the Railway Transport Officer that she must be loaded that night because the train was to start before daylight. There were no shunters to lend a hand, so we pushed a flat truck opposite the platform ourselves and proceeded to drive the car on to it by the light of one hurricane lantern. At last she was securely roped, and we got inside her again and made ourselves comfortable for the night.

In the early hours of the morning we were awakened momentarily by a sharp jolt, but without getting up we went to sleep again. Once or twice we peeped out when the train stopped at stations, but we were not really awake even when it rolled into the Gabbari terminus at Alexandria in the late afternoon. Here we unloaded the car and drove away to the Army Service Corps workshops, where we left her with feelings of relief. Calling a pony gharry, we got into it and sat at our ease, relieved of all responsibility, while the driver took us to an hotel which was patronized by the troops.

Some time before this I had heard from England that three of my civilian friends had been in the S.S. Persia when she was torpedoed in the Mediterranean, but they had landed in Crete and were now in Cairo. Over our tea I discussed with the corporal the possibility of paying them a visit, and he said that as soon as he had discharged his errands in Alexandria he would be very pleased to accompany me. Among other things, we had to arrange for a field kitchen to be sent up to our Battery, and having inspected this ungainly object and received the promise of its keeper to deliver it at the docks in time for it to be loaded on the S.S. Misr, in which we were to sail, we sat down at a cafe and began consuming lemonade and ices. Suddenly I glanced at my watch and sprang into the air like a shot rabbit. The Cairo train was due to leave in ten minutes. We dashed into the road and leapt into a gharry, shouting, 'Cairo Station! Yalla! Yalla!' As we came in sight of the station I saw by the clock that it was three minutes past eleven. The train would leave at five past. Throwing some money at the startled driver we made a run for it, dashing through the station, up the platform, and into the train, where we subsided on cushioned seats, breathless and ticketless, just as it began to move.

It was a first-class compartment, and the Egyptian

gentlemen looked faintly surprised and very supercilious. 'Tickets, please!' was the next scare. The Egyptian gentlemen looked cynically at us. Their looks said, 'Plainly they are travelling first class without authority and without the money to pay. Now they will be thrown out, as they richly deserve.' The pity of it was that our noble fellow-travellers were very nearly right. I would have given all my prospective medals to have been able to produce a ticket to confound them, but I hadn't got one. We fumbled in our pockets, pretending that we had tickets, for the crime of being ticketless in that little boxful of super-ticket-holders seemed enormous. The ticket-inspector's face was like a mask; he stood like a mute, holding out his hand. But when we made false gestures to show him that we had lost our tickets he spoke, gesticulated, and shouted. Then he went away; but I felt inclined to agree with the unspoken opinion of the Egyptian gentlemen that we should be handed over to the police at the first stop. Then along the corridor came a very high official, trimmed with gold braid and a medal or two. He asked to see our tickets in broken English, and I told him that we had none. He told us grimly the amount of the first-class fare and produced a receipt-book and a pencil, and we miserably counted out the money.

On arrival at Cairo we took a gharry at the station and drove through the fine modern streets to the tune of clackety-clack, made by the hooves of the ponies on the asphalt road. We were absorbed in the lively scene when the driver turned his head towards us and asked where we wanted to go. I fumbled excitedly in my pockets, but found I had lost the letter which contained the address of my friends. However, I remembered that the name of the street was Emad ed Din, so we drove there, and after making inquiries of lift-boys, doorkeepers, and numbers of other people in nearly every building throughout its length, we at last found the office of one of my friends.

From that moment our troubles were over. As soon as we

had finished shaking hands with him our host said, 'You're just in time for tea,' and clapping his hands for an Egyptian servant he ordered it to be served at once. We followed him to a luxuriously furnished room, where our feet sank deep in the carpet, and almost immediately Hassan, the servant, dressed in a spotless white gown, with a red sash and a tarboosh, brought in the tray. Our host insisted that we should stay with him at his villa in the suburbs as long as our leave lasted, and as soon as we had finished tea he took us to the office of the other two friends who had been in the Persia with him. Then we all went to Groppi's and other restaurants to listen to the music and eat ices until it was time to go to their house for dinner. We demurred at going into a highly civilized house in our service gear, which had lost all its gloss on the road from Sollum, but they said they would fit us out with white drill suits, such as they were wearing themselves. We were driven to their house in a luxurious car, and later, dressed in spotless, borrowed clothes, we sat down with them to dinner in a room which seemed like an arbour in Paradise after our experiences on the desert. Three Sudanese servants, all dressed in white, with red tarbooshes and sashes, served the most delicious dishes and filled our glasses again and again with champagne. And then I began to discover that our journey to Alexandria, and even in the train coming to Cairo, had been very funny, for our hosts laughed continually as we told them of our adventures.

I woke in astonishment the next morning to find the sun peeping playfully through latticed windows and myself lying in a beautifully soft bed, instead of on the bare ground. Getting out of bed I found myself treading on a silky carpet, and on throwing open the shutters a fairy-like scene of palm trees and flowering shrubs met my delighted gaze.

I dressed in borrowed clothes again, and when we had breakfasted at leisure we all set out for the city, where our friends took us to see the sights, including the Giza Pyramids, the Citadel, the Mosques of Sultan Hasan, Mohammed Ali and others, the Bazaars and the Zoo.

In this fashion the days passed all too quickly, and the time came for us to return to the desert. Having taken a regretful leave of our hosts we got into a wooden-seated third-class carriage of the Alexandria train, and were soon on our way back to duty. That night we slept on the hard ground in a tent at Gabbari Camp, a rough haven for straggling details of the Western Force who wandered from various parts looking for a home and food until such time as they could rejoin their regiments. As I lay down and wrapped my blanket round me I said to the corporal, 'It feels a bit hard after last night!' A strange voice growled, 'Say, what mob do you blokes belong to? The Featherbed Militia or what?'

The next morning we breakfasted off a scrap of tough bacon, stale bread, and tea without milk. Instead of grace a sergeant bawled, 'Everyone will clean up the camp for the C.O.'s inspection, and anyone who tries to dodge it will be put on fatigue. I'm tellin' yer, so get on with it!'

Later we met by chance three men of our Armoured Car Brigade, but belonging to another battery, and as they were completely broke and we had two hundred piastres between us, we gave them one hundred to tide them over their difficulties. In the afternoon we made our way to the docks and went aboard the Misr. She was about to sail, and I searched about quickly to see that the field kitchen had duly been put aboard, but I could not find it anywhere. I begged the Greek captain to delay his ship a few minutes so that I could search the quay, as I supposed the thing must have been delivered there and left. He replied that it was against all regulations and he could not delay, but I had determined to take that kitchen back to Sollum at any cost. 'Keep him talking!' I whispered quickly to the corporal. 'Don't let him break the spell. Shout "Man overboard!" or do anything you like, but keep him off the bridge 'till I come back with the kitchen.'

I jumped down on the quay and rushed along the cargo sheds until I saw the kitchen standing in one of them, with its tall black chimney held up like a beckoning finger. I shouted to some Egyptian porters who were idling near, 'Come on! Lend a hand!' and with their aid I pushed the machine to the ship's side. There we hooked it to a crane, the machinery rattled and screeched, and up she went, to be dropped safely on board to the accompaniment of cheers and laughter. I sprang aboard after her.

We reached Sollum with our prize on Christmas Eve, 1916, and found that some attempt had been made to create a festive atmosphere in the fort. The sergeants' mess was decorated with holly, and even a sprig of mistletoe, and on Christmas Day white paper was laid on the rough mess-tables, mess-tins were polished, and our queer assortment of knives and forks were cleaned up with sand and water. There was ham and fresh vegetables and plum pudding for dinner, and cigars and beer were so plentiful that the football match arranged for the afternoon had to be abandoned. In the evening we sang, talked, drank, and danced to the music of an ancient portable gramophone.

Chapter Eleven
The Siwa Oasis

The pursuit of Ahmed Es Senussi was now to be continued in the Siwa Oasis, and our battery received orders to proceed to that area and assist in cutting off the enemy as they retreated to Jaghbub under pressure of an attack by the Camel Corps and the rest of the armoured cars from Matruh. Later orders, however, were to the effect that the armoured cars only, from Matruh and Sollum, were to make the attack, first concentrating at a point one hundred and eighty miles south of Sollum.

On 1st February 1917 we set out in high spirits, delighted at the prospect of active work again after our long spell of stagnation at Sollum. The Fords were piled high with ammunition-boxes, water fantassis, and a great supply of cases of petrol, bully beef and biscuits, and all the other gear necessary to a modern force. Ahmed and his Senusites had the advantage of us in lightness of baggage, for their weapons and some sacks of corn were all they were encumbered with; and, moreover, the desert, in which we could only exist with difficulty, was their home.

As we left Sollum the place seemed to return to its primitive loneliness, for hardly a sign was now left of the great military force which had once encumbered its beaches, and filled it with bustle and noise. Only the passing nomads would make their temporary camps there now.

We made our first camp at Shekka, and it was almost dark when we arrived there. Some of the party turned their hands to making tea, while the gunners cleaned their weapons anew, and the drivers changed their burst tyres. In a couple of hours all except the guards were asleep in their blankets, lying like corpses on the sand.

At dawn the desert was obscured by mist, but the bustling preparations for departure began without delay. Men scrambled down into the water-hole with empty petrol tins, and crawled clanking along the hidden tunnel to bring up clear water. As soon as breakfast was over we mounted in our cars and proceeded on our way to the southward, reaching the concentration point, where we found the batteries from Matruh, in the afternoon.

Early on the morning of 3rd February a patrol was sent out towards the west to intercept the enemy if he retreated to Jaghbub, while the rest of us, forming the main body, proceeded southward to attack Girba, where the Senusites were believed to be assembled, from the east. After some hours we turned to the west, and passing between some rocky hills came on a blackish surface covered with small, shining stones. The ground appeared to be hard, like that which we had come across so far, but as soon as we got on it there was a severe check, as though powerful brakes had been suddenly applied to our wheels. The surface, in fact, was a thin crust, and the wheels sank through this into soft, red mud. It took us some time and a great deal of trouble to make our way through this to the firm ground beyond.

Our cars were running in pairs: 'Blast' and another were the central pair of the advance guard, and there was a second pair to our right, and a third to our left, but both were out of sight in the undulating ground. Proceeding a little further we came to a descending pass which led into the oasis of Girba itself. We entered this cautiously and slowly wound our way down the rough track between barren hills. The path turned this way and that, and views of side gullies opened up continually as we crept lower and lower towards our objective. Suddenly we were startled by a loud rattle of rifle-fire, and a shower of bullets crashed against the car's armour. My gunner promptly swung his turret round so as to direct his gun in the direction from which the sound had come. I could see no sign of an enemy as I peered through the slit, and I doubt whether he could either, but he elevated his gun and fired a burst at the hill-tops. While he was doing this I threw the engine into reverse gear and backed as quickly as possible round the last bend. Here we reviewed the position, loaded a fresh belt of ammunition into the gun, and steadied ourselves generally. In consultation with the men in the second car we decided that we would take both cars round that bend abreast, as there was room for two at once, and either or both could reverse and run back without looking to see where the other was.

We now moved forward at greater speed than before, and the moment we appeared round the bend the enemy opened on us again, but the gunners in both cars blazed back at them in good style. One belt being empty, my gunner hastened to load another, but before he was ready to fire a rain of bullets struck the car again, and there was a bang, and a hissing from one of the wheels. A tyre had been hit, and as their fire appeared to be too hot to allow us to get any nearer over the difficult ground I ran back in reverse again and waited for the other car to join me under the cover of the slope. Then we drove back a short distance to the advanced base and made our report. As a result of this some of the light Ford patrol cars, with Maxim guns mounted in them, were sent out to keep the enemy's position under fire until nightfall, while a general advance of all the fighting vehicles was ordered for the next day at daylight.

In the early morning we again crept stealthily down the winding track, which in some places was covered with crumbling flakes of loose shale, fallen from the overhanging cliffs. As we proceeded further we came more than once to obstacles which had to be removed with pick and shovel before the cars could advance. We passed the spot at which we had been held up on the day before, without opposition, but as we descended lower and lower the going became worse. Driving down the camel track between those overhanging heights, ignorant of what lay behind the next bend, and in constant expectation of being met with a hail of lead, was nerve-racking work; and presently we began to make a short halt before coming to each turn, so that a man on foot might be sent forward to look cautiously round it and bring us back a report on the condition of the road beyond and whether any of the Senusites were in sight.

We had been advancing on this system for some time, and I was moving towards a bend round which the leading car was just turning after the look-out man had reported all clear, when suddenly there was a loud BOOM! and a shell burst with a crash on the cliff not far above the leading car. The driver was caught in a trap and could not reverse his engine or go forward, for a great cascade of earth and rock fell on his car and half buried it. I stopped 'Blast' dead and saw the driver and gunner of the leading car scramble out unhurt and crawl on their hands and knees to cover.

Luckily their car was not yet round the bend, so we quickly hitched my wire towing-rope to the rear of her chassis and then, reversing my engine, I eased 'Blast' back up the slope until the hawser was taut. The Senusites were apparently satisfied with their efforts, for they held their fire, and a number of our men gathered about the other car and as 'Blast' tugged at the rope they heaved with all their might. At first she seemed to budge a little, but in a moment my wheels began to spin on the loose shale. I saw that if that went on I might get stuck myself, so I stopped my engine and said, 'Let's have another car.' Another car was now hitched onto the back of mine, and with two cars pulling her and half a dozen men pushing we at last managed to pull the stranded car back round the bend. Hardly had we done so when BOOM! went the enemy's gun, and a shell hit the very spot from which we had just pulled her.

Two of our gunners now climbed to the top of the hill on our right so as to try to locate the gun position. It was perilous work, for the cliff was almost perpendicular, but they reached a good observation post and scanned the opposite rocks with their powerful glasses. After a time one of them called down that they could see nothing of the enemy, but that they wanted to haul up one of their machine guns by means of a rope. A rope was produced on the instant and a powerful arm threw it up in a coil. At the second throw the gunner caught the end, and they secured it round a suitable rock. We tied a machine gun to the bottom end and they hauled it up gingerly, helped by another man who clambered up and kept a steadying hand on the rope. Then the tripod was sent up and they mounted the gun. But the enemy still held his fire, and they had no target until they could see the smoke of his gun.

At last it was decided that a light Ford should make a dash round the bend to try to draw his fire, and the car having been selected, its gunner fired a few rounds with his machine gun so as to encourage the Senusites to be on the look-out for him. Then without more ado the Ford was driven forward. Just as it was disappearing round the turn there was another gun-report, and a couple of seconds later another shell crashed into the base of the cliff. It was a narrow escape. Almost at the same moment our machine gun on the hill above burst out into a stabbing splutter. The gunners had found the gun position of the enemy and now blazed away for all they were worth.

We looked at each other inquiringly, understanding that we now had to advance. Somebody went forward to see that the Ford was not blocking the track, and the crews mounted to their places. Then we moved slowly forward. As each car came into view on the bend we expected to hear the report of the gun, and also rifles and machine guns, but there was not a sound. We drove on, tense with expectation, and presently came under the point where we supposed the gun had fired from. My gunner, who was looking through one of his peep holes, said suddenly, 'There it is!' and glancing up through a slit I could just see part of the muzzle of a mountain gun over the top of the cliff. It had evidently been abandoned, and plainly our gunners had found their mark.

The pass now opened out and the cars deployed, each driver intent on finding good going and on searching for any sign of the enemy. It was very difficult to pick up orders given by somebody in another car, and we found that when once we had made contact with an enemy the only way was for each armoured car to be fought independently.

Suddenly we heard firing in the distance. My gunner took a snatch at his gun-belt to make sure that his next cartridge was well home in the breech, and then swung his turret in the direction from which the sound had come. But at that moment a deafening rattle of rifle-fire came from the other side, and a hail of bullets crashed against the armour and the wooden rifle-boxes at the rear. My gunner struggled to bring the turret round again, but it was jammed through the car being at that moment in an inclined position, for she was running sideways on a slope. The gunner swore and muttered, but in a few moments we came on level ground, and there I halted the car. The turret swung round with a jerk and the gunner fell in a heap on top of me. Then I cursed too, and the suppressed excitement in that little steel cylinder was terrific. In another moment the gunner was on his feet again and blazing away at the rocks with a reckless expenditure of ammunition. We had entirely lost count of the position where we had supposed the enemy to be.

Again there was a deafening volley from the side opposite to that at which the gunner was firing, and a yet thicker hail of bullets struck our stationary car. Between us we swung the turret round again, and then I seized my rifle and groped for one of the apertures in the armour, intending to engage the enemy on one side while the gunner kept the others at bay. But I was brought up all standing by a remark of the gunner. 'Hell!' he said. 'They've pierced the gunjacket!' I looked at the gun, which was still dripping water, and then at him. He could not fire the gun without water in the jacket, for the barrel would become red-hot with one burst. 'Come on!' he said. 'Let's have it down quick!' He lifted the gun so as to take its weight, while I pulled out the securing pin, and in a moment we had the gun inside. A bullet had gone right through the jacket, making two holes. 'I've got a piece of soap in my haversack,' I said, and I dived under the dash-plate to get it. Quickly we kneaded the soap into two flat pads, laid one on each of the holes, ripped open a field dressing bandage and bound it round the gunjacket to keep the soap in place. Then my companion grabbed the rubber water-bottle, which was always kept full for the needs of the gun, and poured its contents into the jacket. There was no sign of leakage, so we lifted the gun carefully and remounted it in the turret.

During this operation, which had occupied us only a few minutes, the enemy had not fired a shot at us. Whether they had beaten a retreat or not we did not know, but as none of our friends were in sight and it was already nearly sunset we decided to make our way back to our advanced base. We had come into a narrow place and it was necessary to drive on a little in order to turn the car round; but my companion would not hear of this, so I was obliged to reverse my engine and drive all the way back up the pass lying on one elbow, looking back through a rifle hole in the rear armour door and steering with one hand. In this position I could use only one foot, with which I just managed to reach the clutch lever. I could not operate the foot-brake or the accelerator at all; I set the engine almost racing with the hand-throttle. If it became necessary to brake I had to use the hand brake only, and this I could do by transferring my right hand to it from the wheel, at the same time pressing my body upwards so as to keep the steering locked, to the best of my power. I had often done this before, but never in quite such a narrow and difficult position.

However, I threw myself down and let her go. With half-open throttle she moved backwards shuddering, for it was not easy to make an even start with a fast-revolving flywheel and an almost stationary clutch. We went back very gingerly at first, for I dared not engage the clutch fully until she had more way on her. My gunner murmured nervous remarks of encouragement and appeared to be wishing he had agreed to our going forward to turn, even at the risk of stopping a few of the enemy's shells.

As soon as we started to go back the Senusite sharp shooters opened fire on us again from their hiding places amongst the rocks. We paid little heed to them, however, as the car was pitching and swaying too violently to allow us to return their fire, even if we had wanted to do so. My back was almost at breaking point as we shot madly round bend after bend. Even breathing was difficult, for the clutch was smoking and the fumes of the burning fabric were suffocating. At last my companion, who had been looking through a rifle hole at the rear, announced that we were approaching the corner where we had been shelled on the day before. We could turn with ease here, and in a few moments I stopped the car. I moved into a sitting position with my back against the side and just sat there, completely done. My companion looked at me inquiringly and said, 'This is a fine place to stop in! Another thirty yards and we should be clear of the corner.' But I took little notice of what he said. Nearly all the water had boiled out of the engine and a rest would do the car no harm.

Presently I started her up again, so as to run her back round the bend before turning. As we went round a fierce volley of rifle-fire crashed into our stern, and under the sudden shock I nearly ran her into the rocks. There was a sharp hissing of escaping air and she dropped into a list on one side. One of the rear tires had been shot through. The enemy snipers seemed to be posted at all points of the compass. However, it was now wide enough to turn, so I stopped and then took her forward, bringing her round with her head up the pass, and using the greatest care for fear the other rear tyre should burst under the extra strain.

It was an immense relief to drive forward again, but we were desperately in need of water for the engine, and devoutly hoped that we should soon meet a Ford tender. We were sniped at occasionally, but the enemy offered no target, and we had no intention of getting out of the car and going to look for him, so we saved our ammunition. It was now growing dusk and we made our way back to the advanced base as quickly as we dared to drive the car. Apparently we were the last home, for we found several of our cars moving out to look for us. When we reached camp a great exchange of news took place. One of the cars which had come up against the enemy's main position had fired so much ammunition that the gun water had all boiled away, and they had had to continue the action with rifles until their ammunition had given out too, when they had had to back out and get more. One driver had been wounded in the head by small pieces of a bullet which had struck his guard plate and come through the slits, and he was lamenting that his wound was not a 'Blighty one.'

The unholy din inside the steel cylinder during the action, chiefly caused by the firing of our own gun, was such that weeks passed before I became free of the sense of a continual metallic clanging in my ears. Indeed, most of the men in the brigade were more than half deaf for a long time, and the most frequent words heard in conversation were, 'What did you say?' 'Eh, what's that?' 'Pardon, old boy, I didn't get what you said!'

and similar expressions. Some blamed the speaker for not talking loudly enough, and facetiously told him to make his remarks in the semaphore code.

We learnt that a reconnaissance had already been carried out towards Siwa, which lay to the south-east of where we were; and orders were now issued that the bulk of our force was to proceed there next day.

The night passed without incident, and in the dim light of dawn we rose from the ground, and the ghostly figures of the men could be seen going this way and that, crossing each other continually, as though each was intent on something of great importance which took him in a different direction from that of all the others. The gunners were busily reloading their empty ammunition belts, cleaning guns and rifles, and filling waterjackets. The drivers were filling their petrol tanks and radiators, and starting up their engines. Some turned their crank handles without result, until somebody else said cheerily, 'Hold on, matey! I'll give you a tow,' and ropes were got out for the purpose.

Our orders were to drive straight into Siwa, breaking through any opposition which we might meet. We had not gone far, deployed over a fairly wide front, when rifle bullets began to drop about us fairly frequently; but we kept on steadily, the gunners firing back when ever they could see a target, and eventually we found ourselves in an area where absolute quiet prevailed. I was wondering whether we could have broken through all the opposing force when suddenly, as we rounded a low hill, the morning light revealed an astonishing scene. Along a deep valley cut in the yellow rocks a mass of dark palm trees stretched for mile upon mile to the eastward. This paradise of colour and shadow was the Siwa Oasis.

We had not descended far into the valley when a man dressed in a white robe and waving a white flag was seen coming towards us. A halt was called and the envoy beckoned to us to come near. As he approached he bowed continually and placed his hand to his forehead. Then, through the interpreter, we learnt that the Senusite leader and the remainder of his followers had fled towards the west the day before. Our new friend, one of the notables of Siwa, had come to welcome us to the place in the name of the local sheikhs and the Egyptian Government.

We asked him to ride in with us in one of the cars, and he mounted to a seat on a rifle-box of one of them, and there remained in motionless dignity. The road seen entered between avenues of trees, heavily laden with limes, figs, olives, pomegranates, oranges, lemons, and other fruits; and the rows of date palms extended for miles about us. We drove across quaint little wooden bridges which spanned the irrigation channels of cool clear water, and passed several lakes bordered by green fields and more orchards. Presently we turned into a larger avenue which wound in curves through the groves to our right, and as we still drove on through the silent, peaceful scene we began to meet a few of the peasants. These stared at our travelling forts with wide opened eyes, or turned to fly for their lives; but not the flicker of a smile or of any change of expression crossed the face of our guide. His face remained like a mask as he made a sign with his hand - Right! Left! Straight on! - and he said nothing.

I was almost awed by the richness of the scene into which we had come. Many times on the blazing, thirsty desert I had wondered what these oases were like, and had supposed they were places where there were good wells and a few palm trees growing in the sand. But this was far beyond anything I had ever imagined. We had come out of the wilderness into a veritable Garden of Eden.

We made another turn to the right and suddenly emerged from the trees into a wide expanse of open ground, lit by strong sunlight. And in the distance there lay the queerest town that I have ever seen. It resembled a very large and very ancient ruined castle of giants, in which a swarm of pygmies had made themselves dwellings in the crannies. The flat ground in front of it was treacherous in places, although it looked firm, and I had to put 'Blast' into second and even first gear in order to cross it. Once I stuck, but managed to back out hurriedly. Under the thin surface crust lay salt, slimy mud.

The castle-like town was built of mud, and on its decayed walls tier above tier of little wood-and-mud houses were stuck like swallows' nests. Some of the crumbling mounds looked like huge ant-heaps, swarming with brown human beings instead of ants.

We now halted the cars, and the guide got down and requested our commander to follow him into the town. This he did, accompanied by his staff, and they were met by some more of the chief men of the place as they approached. We watched them conferring together, and the rest of the inhabitants, most of whom had retreated into their hovels, eyed our cars from their windows and doorways. All the vehicles had now drawn up close together, and they must have presented a curious sight to the peepers, whose only previous experience of Europeans had probably been the arrival of a few archeologists and government officials, travelling on camels.

At last our officers returned, and we received the order to drive into the town in single file. Our procession moved slowly through the narrow gaps between the hovels, and finally emerged into an open space, where we drew up in front of a long, low building. This was the Government House, and while we were making an attempt to draw up the cars in line abreast – an attempt which failed on account of the sticky nature of the ground – about a dozen white-robed men came out, bowing and saluting our officers. We got out of the cars and stood to attention as smartly as we could beside them, while the commanding officer and his staff escorted the notables on an inspection of the ill arranged batteries.

The general population had now crept out of their burrows and stood gaping on us from what they may have thought was a safe distance. Soon some of the junior Siwans, naked and dirty, boldly approached close to us and began to maul everything they could lay their little hands on, grinning cheekily at us through the clouds of flies which swarmed around them. We were relieved when the word was given to move out again and pitch our camp on firm ground, where the atmosphere was a little fresher.

The next day we were given a holiday, and those of us who were not on guard wandered away in small groups to inspect the town, followed by the curious glances of all whom we met. In the market-place we found men haggling over huge baskets of dates and olives. The baskets, strong and of various shapes and sizes, were displayed for sale in other shops. The shops were square holes in the mud walls of the houses. Groups of Siwans squatted everywhere, drinking mint tea, talking gutturally, and bargaining with one another for lengths of coarse cloth woven from the hair of animals. There was strange furniture for sale, bedsteads, benches and stools made of wood, with bottoms or seats of woven reeds. The whole place seemed to be a hive of industry; everybody was intently occupied with his own affairs. But for the blend of awful smells I could have remained there for an indefinite time watching the fantastic scene. In one hovel stood the barber, flourishing a razor over the head of his unconcerned customer and shaving him bald as an egg with a few deft strokes. In another place two blind men, naked except for dirty loincloths, walked round and round in a circle, without hurry and without pausing. The scene of their labours was a very greasy and unsavoury hovel, on the floor of which streams of greasy liquid flowed in all directions. The men were harnessed to a long, stout wooden bar which was inserted in a hole in a palm trunk, which had a thread cut on its outer surface. This was fixed in the middle of two large millstones, and the effect of its being turned by the two men was to raise and lower the upper millstone alternately. The contrivance was an olive-press, and the streams of oil which came out of the crushed fruit flowed on to the floor, and from there ran away somewhere in gutters. There were many other curious sights, some of which remained mysteries to me.

On the following day the chief sheikh of the place invited us all to dinner, and when we had duly smartened our appearance, and listened attentively to a lecture by one of the staff officers on Arab etiquette and table manners, we presented ourselves at the old man's house. We were led in through the most luscious and delightful gardens I have ever seen. Winding paths led between masses of beautiful trees, through which the sun cast shafts of light on a green carpet of grass. Following our guide through the sweet-smelling orchards, we presently came to high tunnels of trellised woodwork, covered with vines, from which hung innumerable bunches of fine grapes. At last we came to an open space of soft grass, and in the middle of this the sheikh himself was standing to welcome us. Though tall and stately, he was not fierce-looking and half-contemptuous, as I had expected to find him, but smiled on us in the most kindly and benevolent manner. He stood on no ceremony, but simply spread out both his hands and waved us hospitably to be seated on beautiful carpets which had been laid for us on the grass; and these simple actions of his were as expressive as any words. When we were all seated he clapped his hands, and at once two giant black slaves or servants made their appearance, carrying between them a great copper dish on which was the sizzling carcass of a whole sheep, brown as a berry and done to a turn, resting on a small mountain of white, boiled rice, every grain of which was separate and whole. Round the whole sheep were ranged parts of others - legs, shoulders, heads, and so on - all looking so beautifully cooked that our mouths watered at the sight. Other servants followed behind, carrying bowls of melted butter, olives, cucumbers, and other vegetables and condiments.

Reverently the big black men set down their lovely burden in front of us. Etiquette was almost as completely forgotten as bully beef and biscuits, and it was with difficulty that we restrained ourselves from falling like famished wolves on that glorious dish, the aroma of which came tantalizingly floating under our noses. However, without delay or ceremony our host advanced to the great dish, beckoning to us to do likewise, and sank on one knee, signing to us to seat ourselves on the carpeted ground. As many of us as could squeeze in took station accordingly; the others had to wait for the arrival of a second dish, which was brought forth immediately after the first, I believe, though I was much too busy to see it. The servant now poured a golden stream of melted butter over our sheep and its bed of rice, and as soon as he had emptied the bowl our host took a handful of the rice, squeezed it into a ball in the palm of his hand and slipped or threw it neatly into his mouth. He next took up a morsel of meat and bolted this too. Then he smiled round on us, waved his hand slightly, and seemed to say, 'Fall to, gentlemen!' The little ceremony had taken only a minute, but by this time we were worked up to fever pitch, and our mouths were aching to begin their work. The fat of the land lay heaped up before us: we had not eaten such food for weeks; we had not had such appetites for years, if ever; and a second's delay seemed like an hour. With a lusty roughness we fell on the food, grabbing up great handfuls of savoury rice, tearing great pieces of tender, juicy meat off the sheep and gulping it down ravenously. Our host nodded and smiled round at us, evidently pleased with our undisguised appreciation of the delicious fare he had provided for us. Now and then he clapped his hands and gave an order to the servant, who at once ran to receive his injunctions, and in obedience to them poured into the dish more melted butter or added further bowls of vegetables to the feast.

The food in the dish dwindled as our belts became tighter, and gradually, one by one, we edged back and reclined on the edge of the carpet or on the grass and gazed up, replete with food and contentment, at the green foliage overhead. When the last of us had finished eating, and nobody could any longer respond to the sheikh's smiling gestures to eat more, the dishes were removed. But hardly had the carpet been cleared when our now lazy eyes were again dazzled and aroused by another beautiful sight: the two black giants were carrying towards us an enormous bowl filled and heaped up with the choicest fruits. This aroused us from our contented lethargy, and we moved into line again. I took a pomegranate and asked my neighbour what was the best way to eat it, but he could not tell me. One of the watching servants, however, saw my difficulty almost at once, and taking the fruit gently from my hand he rolled it between his own for a moment, snipped the top off with his knife and handed it back to me. Instead of being hard it was now soft, as though filled with pulp. I was still mystified about the way it should be eaten, and seeing this the smiling servant took another pomegranate from the dish, kneaded it, cut off the top and then took a suck at the opening he had made. Imitating his action I found that the juice flowed, cool and seedless, like wine out of a glass, leaving little inside the skin but seeds.

We stayed in that pleasant glade for several hours, and were unwilling to leave it; but at last we felt that etiquette forbade us to remain any longer, so we took our leave with hearty thanks and compliments to our host.

Chapter Twelve
Farewell To The Western Desert

Our campaign seemed now to be over, and our thoughts turned to finding some means of amusing ourselves. In several parts of the oasis there were very ancient burial grounds, with tombs dating from the days of the Pharaohs, and before long we were attacking some of these tombs with picks and shovels, as an organized excavation-party. We found ourselves unable to open most of those we tackled, as our tools were not equal to the task; but presently we discovered one which was closed by a stone slab which had become loose. We spent a whole day in loosening this further, and at last, under the pressure of our levers, it fell away with a crash. Eagerly we squeezed into the dark chamber with a lamp, and there we found a great sarcophagus. The walls of the chamber were decorated with hieroglyphic inscriptions, and it was queer to find these in perfect preservation after perhaps several thousands of years.

On the outside of this tomb the name Ehrenberg was carved roughly, and I heard that this had been done by one of the two or three European explorers who had reached Siwa after great difficulties. I believe Ehrenberg's expedition visited the place in 1820. It was our intention to go on with our excavating, but the fates decreed otherwise, for our doctor discovered that malaria and worse diseases were rife in the oasis, and that it was dangerous for us to remain there. We were therefore ordered to move out to the high desert again.

We turned our backs on this little paradise with regret and drove out in a long column to our old concentration point, from which we had started for the attack on Girba and Siwa.

Here we were ordered to make a permanent base, surrounded by trenches and barbed wire entanglements. It was not a spot which had any natural beauty or interest, for there was nothing to be seen anywhere except the ring of the horizon. Between that circle and us the desert was perfectly flat and empty. Here in the shadeless wilderness we prepared to be grilled like bits of steak in a frying-pan all the spring and summer. In the hot midday hours we crawled under tents, tarpaulins or cars, but none of these things seemed of much use to keep out the heat and sand, even in February.

Every week a supply column of Ford cars ran to Mersa Matruh and back, three days out, one day's rest at Matruh, and three days back. This was the working week of their drivers, who were lucky to have their day's rest at Matruh and not in the desert with us. We used to run sweepstakes on the time of their arrival, the man who guessed the nearest getting the prize. Most of us tried to malinger in one way or another, but with little success. At last, however, I hit upon a scheme which seemed to promise good results. I explained carefully to our commanding officer that all the cars were badly in need of repair. 'What! All of them?' he cried. 'Yes,' I said, 'all of them. But of course some are more in need of it than others.' He decided that the vehicles must go to Matruh in pairs and be thoroughly overhauled, and gave orders for the first pair to leave, and to return as quickly as possible so that two others might be sent.

Five days later two very travel-stained armoured cars, 'Blast' and 'Bloodhound,' reached Matruh in the evening dusk. Their crews had only one idea, which was to get rid of them. As soon as they had turned them over to the workshop engineers they intended to spend their time between sleeping and lying in the blue water of the Mediterranean.

The next morning I left my quarters in high spirits and turned my face towards the sea, but I had not gone many steps when an orderly rushed out of the stone block-house which was used as an orderly-room and called me back. 'These are orders for you,' he said, and handed me a paper. I glanced at the typewritten message. At the head was my name, among others, and underneath the words, 'You will report to Alexandria at the earliest possible date.' There were further instructions about the disposal of the two cars, about drawing rations and so on; but my thoughts flew back to my comrades of the Brigade marooned in their little ring of entrenchments and wire out on the lifeless plain. I should never see that place again, nor the many other nameless spots of earth where we had sweated and fought together.

Chapter Thirteen
Lawrence

At Alexandria four of us from the Duke of Westminster's Brigade joined a number of others from various fronts, and the whole party were then detailed to take charge of eight armoured cars and two Rolls-Royce tenders. The latter were 'Blast' and 'Bloodhound,' which had been converted at Alexandria. Early in August 1917 we entrained with these for Suez, at which port we remained for two weeks without receiving further orders. During that time Suez was full of rumours; there had been a large number of British troops here, and later a detachment of French mountain artillery had arrived, but all had dispersed again without clear rhyme or reason. Yet there were hints that some sort of campaign was going on in the Arabian desert. To us it seemed that the authorities were in a state of indecision about what to do with us, until, towards the end of August, we received orders to load the cars on a ship in the harbour. As soon as all were aboard and the gangways removed she steamed out into the Gulf and down the coast of Sinai, and we knew that we were bound for Arabia.

Before the war the Arabs of the Hedjaz had asked for British help to throw off Turkish rule; but there is a time encouraging revolution, as for everything else, and that time had not then come, so far as England and Arabia were concerned. When Turkey declared war the Sheriff of Mecca thought the hour had come, and some of our responsible men agreed with him, while others did not. There was more benevolence than disapproval for his plans, but much less active help than promises. The latter, like most English promises, were fairly reliable, as political promises go, but they were really promissory notes, things that had to mature a bit. The Sheriff, simple man, thought they were a cash-down sort of undertaking, and he began his revolt all alone. This seemed well enough at first to the people in Whitehall, and even to many in Cairo. They probably had visions of masses of Arabs swarming out of the desert, like bees out of a hive, and beating Turkey by sheer numbers, while the British Army looked on during its spare time between sports meetings. It would all be beautifully cheap and easy.

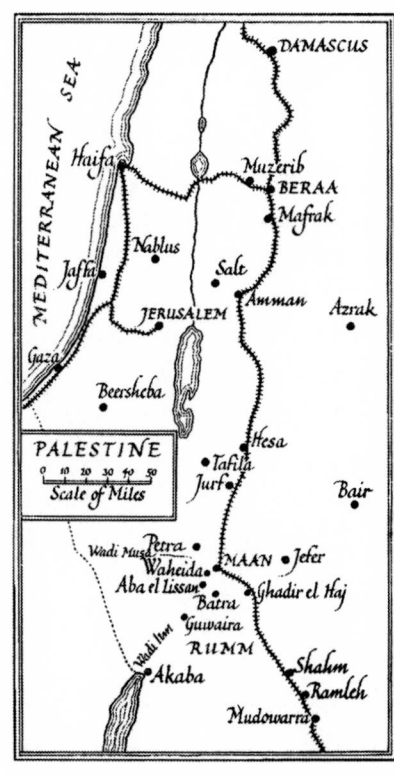

Palestine.

But a pious old gentleman with a strong tendency to swollen head, even if he is the chief living descendant of a prophet, may not be a fit leader of revolution. Hussein began to give himself titles and to take a keen interest in forcing the pace of the Turkish brass band which his revolutionaries had captured in the lump. While those wilting captives blew and blew in Mecca, growing shabbier day by day, for the old man's amusement, the revolutionary army went home to its tents, or sat down in the more comfortable oases. True, Mecca and Jedda had been relieved of Turkish rule, but Medina, garrisoned by fifteen thousand Turkish regulars, commanded by a real soldier, Fakhri Pasha, lay between the Arab rabble and the British Army which they were supposed to help to conquer Palestine.

127

In Cairo it was realized that something had to be done to invigorate the Arabs, and several officers were sent to Jedda to make more promises, and to arrange for redeeming some of the earlier ones. This was in the summer of 1916, and by the time our armoured car unit reached Akaba, late in August 1917, the Arab campaign was beginning to be organized in the European style. The organization never got much beyond a beginning, which partly accounts for the success of the campaign.

After rounding the point of Sinai, our steamer anchored at the head of the Gulf of Akaba, and we set about hoisting the ten heavy cars out of her hold and moving them up the beach. The only way by which we should be able to get them up to the plateau of the interior was through the pass of Itm, a narrow corridor between high rock mountains. Its sandy bottom was obstructed by great rocks which had fallen from the cliffs, and before we could hope to drive through it we had several months' hard work before us. This we began without delay. We blasted the larger rocks in pieces with gelignite, threw aside the smaller ones, and overlaid with broken shale those parts where there was deep sand. The work became harder as we progressed, for the further we went the larger were the masses of fallen stone and the narrower the pass. From the start the heat was so great that we were unable to begin work until about five o'clock in the afternoon. The bends in the gorge made it appear as though we were imprisoned between walls hundreds of feet high, and the explosions of the blasting charges echoed there like artillery fire.

When our day's work was finished we crawled under a tarpaulin stretched between two of the cars at the cleared end of the pass, and there an ancient gramophone entertained us with a screeching of worn-out music. Every three or four days we moved our camp a little further into the gorge. Only when work was in progress was our existence tolerable; in the silence of the midday heat a feeling of loneliness, accompanied by a curious reticence of speech, seemed to settle on everybody. Yet we all huddled together under the tarpaulins, like men seeking for warmth or sympathy.

Lying under this cover I was forever trying to think out what our task was to be, when this navvy work was completed, if it ever was. The lack of information, and even of rumours, was extraordinary. A certain captain with whom I spoke about the matter mumbled something about the danger of the job – that it was all a kind of experiment, that it might develop into an important campaign, that perhaps it would be unsuccessful. I tried to find some meaning in these burblings, but without result. Some of these regular officers were much worse off than I was, for they seemed to have no work to do; and I know now that many of them were quite out of their element in circumstances where drill-book rules could not be applied usefully, if at all. They were the organizers, and they were finding it difficult even to begin organizing rocks and sand, and a truculent lot of scallywags who were here today and gone tomorrow.

Meanwhile, we continued to organize the Itm gorge. When the sun had sunk somewhat, a stir of life announced that the Egyptian labour gang, who did the heaviest work, were being urged back to their task by the foreman with his whip. Whether the grinning navvies suffered more than the sweating foreman from their exertions is doubtful. Certainly the men did not wince under the lash, though their taskmaster simmered continually in a subdued frenzy. Someone would start our gramophone so as to rouse us to get up and join in the work; another would throw a boot at it, with a grumbling curse.

In three weeks we progressed about ten miles with great exertions, and always when we looked ahead it seemed to us impossible that we could ever make a road fit for cars to pass there. My job was to mark those rocks which would need to be blasted, and ahead of me there were others who had to mark out the limits of the track for the road, and within which my work lay.

One day when we had reached this stage I was surveying my progress as I rolled a cigarette of tobacco dust, when Hassan, the Egyptian foreman, pointed out to me with his long rhinoceros-hide whip a group of dishevelled Arabs, mounted on richly harnessed camels, who were riding slowly down the pass, picking their way between the stones. 'Arab no good!' he said bitterly. 'Thief!' and he spat on the ground in disgust. Like many peasants and town Arabs he hated and feared the desert men.

'Yalla! Imshi! Clear off!' I shouted to the first of the Arabs, who was making his camel kneel.

He paid no heed, so I swung my hands at him, palms forward, as one shoos chickens. He had left his camel now, and seeing me doing this he hastened towards me, which struck me as strange. Looking now, for the first time, full into his eyes, I had a shock. They were steel grey eyes, and his face was red, not coffee-coloured like the faces of other Arabs. Instead of the piercing scowl there was laughter in those eyes. As he came close I heard a soft, melodious voice, which sounded girlish in those grim surroundings, say, 'Is your captain with you?' He spoke in the cultivated Oxford manner. I dropped my cigarette in sheer astonishment. 'Who the . . . ? What the . . . ?' I stammered out.

He placed his hand for a moment on my shoulder. 'My name is Lawrence,' said he, 'I have come to join you.

I had never heard of Lawrence. Who had? Nobody knew what he had done or was doing, except Allenby and one or two of the senior officers who were his nominal superiors in the Arab zone. But this unexpected meeting meant more to me than the most sensational and true reports could have meant. The effect his arrival had on me was extraordinary. During all the aching boredom and labour of the past three weeks I had said to myself, again and again, that if only I knew something of what it was I was working for, something of the object for which I supposed we should presently fight, I could have worked with ten times the willingness and ten times the ease. In this moment my carking anxiety and the feeling of purposelessness and of boredom left me completely, and I never knew it again throughout the war. My first sight of Lawrence brought me ease and happiness, a most satisfying feeling that my little labours had a purpose, and a fine one.

Thus mentally transfigured, it was some moments before I realized that I must reply to him, answer his question. 'Is your captain with you?' he had asked me. I heard myself say in a strange voice, 'Will you come this way, sir.'

I led him towards the captain's tent, while the other chaps stared at me and my Arab with goggling eyes. I spoke into the tent and then stood back and stared like an awestruck child at my companion. He returned my glance, smiling serenely with a friendly humour; and then the captain came out. He showed no surprise, and they shook hands like old friends. I backed away, still staring at the little Arab with the quiet voice standing there by the tent. The spell was not quite broken until I stumbled over something, and then I turned away and went back to my work in the gorge. There everybody bombarded me with questions, but I could tell them no more than what they had already seen for themselves.

The remainder of the group of Arabs stood or sat idly where Lawrence had left them. The richness of their saddles and the appearance of breeding about their camels made it clear that they had some special status, and I learnt later that they were Lawrence's permanent bodyguard. Among them were Farraj and Daud, those two impish youths who would never be parted from one another, and whose desire was to follow their leader through all dangers. They stood carelessly throwing stones in competition, then chased one another round and round the camels, and finally fell together in a heap, laughing boisterously.

All these men had been carefully chosen for their fighting qualities. Some of them had the blood-price hanging over their heads, or had been banished from their own tribes for some unpardonable crime. Such men are the least likely to depart at the call of family feeling.

One of my comrades remembered to have seen Lawrence at Wejh, for he had been one of those in charge of two armoured cars which had earlier been sent to that place. They had made many attempts to drive inland in support of the Arab bands, but the country had always defeated them by reason of the large tracts of loose sand there. Time and again they had attempted to follow the mob of Arabs, but they had always been balked by some obstruction. Once his car stuck immovably in the sand, sixty miles inland. The only thing they could do was to lighten her by stripping all her armour off and leaving it in the desert. This they did, and then, with the bare chassis, they managed to get back to Wejh. There a small and apparently unimportant Englishman, in Arab headdress and English officer's uniform, had spoken to him words of sympathy in his bad luck, and of warm congratulation on bringing back the important part of his car. He had not talked about danger, experiments, or failure, but had told my pal that he was to return to Egypt with the chassis and re-equip it for the advance which was being planned. This sort of confidence and human decency being rare between officer and man in the British Army, my pal had at first been a little bewildered; but afterwards, on thinking of the matter, he had felt impressed, I gathered, with a sort of gratitude, and now, on being brought in contact with Lawrence again, his feeling amounted to devotion. Up till this time he and I had been comrades; now we became friends, and so we remained until, some months later, death parted us in this same Itm gorge.

Lawrence came out of the tent and mounted his famous Ghazala; the thirty camels rose with their riders, and then they all moved out of sight round a bend in the pass.

A new cheerfulness filled our camp that night, and instead of lying down in glum silence, as we had grown used to doing, we sat late round the fire, talking and speculating on the amusement which was coming to us. The next day our captain shed a little more dim light on our affairs, telling us briefly that we were here to serve Colonel Lawrence, and that his commands must be obeyed smartly and in a soldier-like manner. I suppose he thought that because Lawrence was dressed in Arab clothes he might find it difficult to exact prompt obedience; in the army a man's clothes are so often the only sign of his authority. It was already amusing to me to think of Lawrence as a severe military colonel. In our corps, as in others, orders were snapped out like curses, and salutes to officers were exacted in the fullest measure. The orders were passively obeyed, the salutes were yielded. Lawrence's orders were directions, and he cared nothing about saluting, except that he preferred to dispense with it. Instead of an order, he usually seemed to raise, first of all, a question for discussion; giving the impression, a true one, that he wanted to have one's opinion of what was best, before he decided on the course to be followed. Some, whose opinion had never been sought by an officer before, looked dumbfounded at him. For the moment it was beyond their power of understanding that this man, who knew the desert and its inhabitants so well, should actually ask them for suggestions. Very frequently one's remarks seemed to influence his final directions. These were carried out eagerly by all, and by those who had not known him long he was saluted with alacrity. Some years after the war he expressed in a letter to me his relief that the 'sir business' was dead and buried so far as we were concerned. Smartness was his very last quality. I saw him in military uniform only once, and he looked almost awkward in his untidiness.

In two weeks more we had completed our road and could survey it with pride. It seemed to us that it must compare very favourably with the work of the Royal Engineers. Our officers, swelling visibly with zeal to report to some noble brass-hat what had been done, went off to find one at Akaba.

Soon we should see whether our road was fit to stand the passage of the eight heavy armoured cars. I had already tested it with 'Blast,' my Rolls-Royce tender. She had come up it in magnificent style, and the order had gone to Akaba for the armoured cars to move forward. At the furthest end of the gorge we waited in our camp for their appearance.

At Alexandria, where her armoured body had been removed, 'Blast' had been fitted with a low, sporting body, set in streamline with her long bonnet. Thus lightened, she answered to her accelerator, when on firm going, like a shell coming out of a gun. Two spare wheels, mounted on brackets at the rear, insured her against disablement by tyre trouble; and I had had two short, strong running-boards with tapered ends fitted to her, equipped with quick-release wing screws. These easily detached boards would serve at need to make a temporary bridge over small gullies, or for use in deep sand. Then, mounted in special brackets, so that they lay on the running-boards, there were two four-inch sectioned poles, the uses of which were two. They were made to the length which would allow them to be manipulated between the front and rear wheels, and one end, cut so that it was V-shaped in section, could be forced under the rear wheel and between its two tyres when the car became bogged in deep sand. The other end having been pushed down under the running-board, a firm inclined track was made for the wheel, and when this had been done on both sides, all was ready for driving forward. As the wheels revolved they moved along the poles, and forced them level with the ground. If all went well it was often possible to secure enough momentum on this short, solid track to carry the car over the immediate obstruction. The process was certainly laborious, and we often had to do it scores of times in one stretch of sand, but without this simple apparatus the mobility of the cars would have been very much reduced. The second use of the poles was for making a solid base on soft ground when it was necessary to use the jack.

The day came when the silence of the pass was shattered by a metallic clanging. The noise grew louder and louder, and suddenly, round the last bend, charged the first of our armoured cars, roaring in low gear and hissing steam like a railway engine. Another appeared, and then another, and soon the narrow gorge seemed filled with the stream of them, rocking and pitching in great style. We gave them a cheer and then ran to point out to the drivers suitable places in which to pull up.

When they came to a standstill I saw Lawrence sitting on the rifle-box of the first of them, with Major Marshall, our doctor, opposite to him. They jumped down, and I noticed with surprise that Lawrence's feet were entirely bare. He had not even sandals. 'Good lord!' I exclaimed, 'how can you possibly walk on these sharp stones, sir?'

'Just practice,' he answered quietly.

Both he and the doctor, who was also a very nice man and popular with the men, seemed delighted with their trip, and it was evident that they enjoyed one another's company.

There were other officers in the cars too. Our captain had found a good supply of brass-hats. Colonels and majors there were in plenty, and, all told, I believe there were as many officers as rank and file in the British details of the Arab expedition at this time. The people who gave orders were so numerous that it was quite a privilege to be among those who only received them. As time went on the importance of rank fell into abeyance, and with it much of the distinction between European and Asiatic, for there were among us a number of Turkish ex-officers, now converted into Arab officers, some of them of high rank. About this time Jaafar Pasha, captured at Agagia, was released from the Cairo Citadel and made commander-in-chief of a large part of the Arab levies.

We soon ceased to look like regulation soldiers. Instead of uniform we wore ragged drill shorts and shirts, open at the neck, with the Arab kefiya on our heads and heavy army boots on our sockless feet. We were the worst-looking soldiers in the British Army, and this was the outward sign of our fitness to do the work we had in hand.

We refilled the hot and nearly empty radiators, and the officers gathered about Lawrence. While their discussion went on we straightened out the column and I drew up my tender at its head, while the other was stationed at the rear. At last our captain came towards me, accompanied by Lawrence.

'You will take Colonel Lawrence,' he said.

I saluted and was delighted. Lawrence looked my 'Blast' over with a critical glance, and asked me several questions as to her powers of acceleration, speed, and so on. It was plain that he enjoyed the very sight of a fast-moving machine. We got in and I let in the clutch, and as we rode side by side he talked freely. It would be foolish to say that he talked without reserve, for such a man is always full of the power of reserve; but the effect he produced on one was of complete confidence. Every remark and every question was full, unhesitating, and clear. It was the first time I had ever been told facts frankly by an officer, and I began to feel in the swim of things and full of the keenness which understanding of one's task brings. He explained to me much about the Arab revolt, its beginnings and its progress, and then he discussed with me the great job which lay ahead of us. He was full of confidence, but he treated me to none of the false optimism of 'general orders.' He spoke of the difficulties he had had with the Arabs and with our own people, of his fortunate chances, of his misgivings as to the future conduct of those with whom he had to negotiate, and he spoke a little, a very little, of those far reaching political hopes of his for the Arabs

We left the gorge of Itm far behind us.

Chapter Fourteen
Feisal

After travelling for about forty miles on firm going we came over the plateau to the plain of Guweira, where we encountered sand-dunes and hummocks topped with clumps of camel grass. I had some difficulty in choosing a level path for all my wheels at once, and the belt of the loaded machine-gun, which was mounted on its tripod in the middle of the tender, flew and whacked here and there in a dangerous manner. The armoured cars ground along behind us, and with them were the Ford transport cars, loaded chiefly with ammunition and fantassis.

At Guweira I had solid evidence of some of the information which Lawrence had given me as we came along. The tents of an army extended right round the rock which gave the place its name, and stretched away in the distance; and in the midst of them was the tent of the figurehead of the Arab revolt, Feisal, son of the Sheriff Hussein. The troops consisted of Bedouin Arabs, Iraqis, Syrians, Sudanese, and a few Turks. As we drove towards the rock the whole army seemed to come out of its tents, and Arab horsemen, riding bare-back, galloped round and round us furiously, with flying cloaks and brandished rifles, crying out of their throats, 'Ya Aurans! Ya Aurans!' as though the name of my companion was a battle-cry.

We made our camp near the rock - the distance from Akaba was about sixty miles - and Lawrence passed through the enthusiastic rabble to Feisal's tent. As the sun sank behind the distant hills fires began to flicker in the encampments, putting reflected sparks into the eyes of the Arabs who sat about them.

Some of the men baked bread in thick, flat cakes in the red embers, others spoke gutturally to each other, drained little coffee cups, or smoked pipes with stone bowls. I moved cautiously amongst the tents, not wishing to attract attention as an intruder. I had seen nothing like this camp, in the Libyan Desert or elsewhere. Here was the real Arab, the born fighter who thrived only by the power of his sword. The guttural voices were everywhere, all arguing, apparently, and all endeavouring to argue at once, till the night was full of their hoarse babbling. Then, as I was becoming seriously afraid that blood would be shed amongst some group I was watching, they would suddenly all appear to collapse in laughter, and each would slap his neighbour on the back with affectionate joviality. The coffee-cups circulated continually.

A War Consultation Of Arab Sheikhs At Guweira.

Presently I came to two tall black sentries, standing on guard outside a great tent, brightly lit inside. I concealed myself in a point of vantage and stared with all my eyes. There before me, in the light of the flares, was the Emir Feisal, sitting on his rich carpet. His face was pale, almost like old ivory in that light.

Gold sword hilts and daggers shone at the belts or in the hands of those who sat with him, and all wore long gowns of silk and flowing robes of camel hair. All this was spread under the indigo sky and the flashing stars, and I felt that I was actually looking at a scene like those in The Arabian Nights. I half believed, and very much hoped, that I should see lovely princesses of Arabia if I remained there on watch.

At the Emir's right hand a small figure sat amongst the great sheikhs of the tribes. They were all looking at him, and one after another putting questions to him, grave and gay. It was Lawrence, clearly engaged in one of those conferences of his, in which he had to explain to the Arabs that their chance of getting what they wanted depended on discipline as well as bravery. It is fortunate that he had plenty of gold to drug them with, or even he might not have been able to manipulate them to his will.

Opposite to Lawrence sat Auda, the great sheikh of the Howeitat tribe, and one of the most famous warriors in all Arabia. I saw his fierce face first in profile: the piercing eye, the thin aquiline nose, the bearded chin stuck out in haughty defiance.

As fast as these plied Lawrence with questions he answered them gravely, patiently, and promptly, without turning a hair. At last they all stirred, rose, and taking Feisal's hand in turn they began to go away into the night. I turned quickly from the scene and made my way towards the cars, five hundred yards away. The moonlight falling on their turrets showed them like a flotilla of submarines, half submerged in dark waters, ready to strike. It would be hard to say which was the more striking of these Arabian Nights scenes, that which I had just left or the one which I now saw.

A sentry challenged, 'Who goes there?'

I hissed, 'It's all right, Gink. It's only me.'

'Is . . . that . . . so,' drawled Gink the Canadian. 'Pass, friend. Bob's your uncle.'

I found my way to the Rolls-Royce, and stretching myself on her front seat I placed my head on the accumulator box. This made a reasonably comfortable couch, and it was to be my bed for the next eighteen months.

Dawn revealed the tents of our army in a haze. The troops were preparing to move, and there was a great noise of feeding and grooming the animals, of hooves on the stones, and the whining and frisking of stallions. To this was added the continuous babel of Arabic speech.

By degrees most of the army got on their horses and camels, and then they made some attempt to form in line. But both the men and the animals were unused to the discipline of the West, and their line was a mere broken zigzag. In a few minutes a group of their officers rode out from behind one of the larger tents and approached the line, evidently bent on inspecting it in due form. I looked casually at the chief of these, who was riding ahead of the rest. Then I looked again, staring hard. I gripped the arm of a man standing near me; he was startled and tried to shake me off. 'Look!' I exclaimed.

'Look at what?' he said brusquely.

'That's Jaafar Pasha!' I cried, amazed. 'I know him well. We captured him near Sollum and sent him to Cairo. He was leading the Senussi against us!'

Then my eye fell on another of them. 'Good God! And there's Nuri Bey!' I cried. 'The cunning dodger! Now, what's the game here?'

More than once I had chased Nuri on his piebald horse in the Libyan Desert, and but for his clever choice of ground I should certainly have caught him. How these two had managed to reach their present station was a mystery to me. I felt an

141

impulse to rush to Lawrence and confide my great discovery to him. I thought he could surely not be aware of who those two men were. There were still two of my Libyan comrades with us who could corroborate my statements. However, I resolved to do nothing rash, but to keep my news until I saw how the land lay.

I learnt later that Jaafar had tried, in fact, to get out of the Citadel at Cairo by shinning down a blanket hung over the wall, but he had dropped off too soon in the darkness and injured his foot. He was easily caught, as he was unable to put his foot to the ground, and later, when he heard of the Arab revolt, he offered his services to Feisal and was accepted. Although an officer in the Turkish army, Jaafar was an Arab of Baghdad. Nuri's case was a little different, as he was half a Turk and was closely related to Enver Pasha.

I was delighted that Lawrence had singled out my tender for his own use, and from that time until the end of the campaign we travelled together something like twenty thousand miles. Until then he had ridden the length and breadth of northern Arabia on camels, outstaying the Bedouins themselves in his disregard of hunger and fatigue. But there was no comparison between Ghazala and a Rolls-Royce in the mind of a man who the quicker he could shoot himself from end to end of the desert like a weaver's shuttle, the better he would be pleased. He could not have controlled the Arabs by telephone, even if he had been connected with their various shifting camps. The only influence of any use at all amongst them is direct personal influence. They were widely scattered, and the nearer he could get to being everywhere at once the better it would be. There were still times when Ghazala or her sisters could be of use to him, but very largely from this time onwards the Rolls-Royce, later aided by an occasional aeroplane, took her place.

From his first arrival in Arabia Lawrence managed the revolt almost alone. Without him there is little doubt that Feisal would have made terms with the Turks; and as for the British, none of them believed that much would come of his efforts, not even his nearest colleagues and friends. Their attitude was that although he would probably fail to produce any direct help for the army in Palestine, his activities might, with luck, prevent many of the Arab tribes from joining the enemy. After his extraordinary capture of Akaba, in July 1917, however, their views altered, and Allenby's support made his success certain.

On the day after our arrival at Guweira Lawrence decided to make his first raid by car on the Turkish railway. We loaded the two tenders with a large supply of gun-cotton, a week's rations and water, a case of five thousand sovereigns marked 'Commonwealth Bank of Australia,' several coils of electric cable, a battery exploder, and several other articles which had been found useful on previous demolition raids.

Lawrence, Nuri, and I filled the front seat of the first car. Both vehicles had machine guns mounted on a tripod in the centre of the platform. The gunner's seat was in the rear. There were several rifles strapped in convenient places, and we all carried loaded revolvers. Lawrence was dressed in a brown Arab cloak trimmed with gold, and a white headdress with silk rope and tassels. Nuri wore a khaki tunic and breeches, with boots and leggings, and the kefiya. Nuri's headdress was bound about his head like a turban, and looked for all the world like a great nest with a speckled bird in it, moulting feathers. The fringe made the feathers. My headdress was a discoloured square piece of khaki cloth, kept on with a greenish rope, which, through continual pulling on and off, had come to resemble a length of ancient bootlace. As we drove away from Guweira the gunners of the armoured cars were turning their guns so that they pointed towards the tents of the Arabs. They had charge of the gold and the explosives, and were not minded to give our allies the benefit of a very strong doubt as to their honesty in all circumstances.

With a snort of the open exhaust I plunged out on a trackless course towards the distant hills, dodging and twisting between the hummocks, some of which were as large as beehives. In a few moments the clouds of white dust thrown up by the double wheels hid the rock of Guweira from sight. The other tender, 'Grey Knight,' came behind us at a distance and in echelon, so as to keep clear of our dust. So we plunged ahead, like two ships in a rough sea, flinging up spray as we went.

My passengers remained silent for some time, and I began to think they were not much impressed by motoring in the desert. I had become thoroughly accustomed to bucketing over rough ground, but probably they preferred camels. However, presently Lawrence murmured, 'Splendid!' and smiled from the folds of his headdress. At this I expressed a hope that the going would improve before long, and soon he was exchanging camel-yarns for my car-yarns.

Nuri was obviously listening, although he did not understand English, and every now and then I shot a glance at him, thinking of our moves and counter-moves in Libya. Presently Lawrence noticed my interest in the Turk, and I related to him something of my service before coming to Arabia. When I had done he spoke to Nuri, and at once the Turk's face took on a new look of alertness, and he babbled quickly in Arabic. 'Ask him if he remembers Bir Wair, where he only just managed to escape our armoured cars on his piebald horse,' I said to Lawrence. Yes, he remembered that well. 'A burst tyre saved him,' I said. One of the many questions Nuri put to me, through Lawrence as interpreter, was, 'Who gave information about the location of the Tara prisoners?' As he was on our side now I told him, and when I congratulated him on the run he and Jaafar had given us for their money he beamed with pleasure. We were all on the best of terms. I nudged Lawrence. 'Tell Nuri this is the very car in which I chased him,'

I said. That brought a look of incredulous surprise, and then roars of laughter, in which we all joined.

Having reached this stage of familiarity with the commanders of our army, I discreetly turned my whole attention to driving and lapsed into silence. Presently Lawrence, who was directing me, said we were heading for Rumm. Suddenly the car foundered in deep sand, overgrown with tall reeds and brushwood. I had been caught napping, and we had crashed through the scrub at no great speed with the engine in top gear, and already gasping. However, we pulled out at last without having to make use of the poles, and then came on a perfectly flat and hard surface. It was a dry rainpool, surrounded by jagged rocks, and between these we ran easily, our wheels scarcely leaving the faintest mark on the caked surface. Some of the rocks were like the walls of ancient buildings, very interesting and beautiful to see. Between their perpendicular sides there were narrow alleys, and in some of them there were caves which had the appearance of windows and doors. Some of the pinnacles rose to nearly a thousand feet, and the whole place had the mysterious charm of magnificent ruins. We purred smoothly through this stately ring of walls in silent procession, and speechless with wonder I glanced at my companion. 'And this is Rumm,' murmured Lawrence.

We rounded in silence a tall cliff which rose to a dizzy height, and for a long time we went on and on through this enchanted region. Finally we emerged on an open plain, hard and dead level as a yellow billiard table; and here we drew up the cars side by side. The Howeitat Arab Zaal, and Colonel Joyce, came from the other car to confer with Lawrence and Nuri. One of the chief objects of our expedition was to make observations for use in planning an attack by Jaafar's force on Mudowarra, a station on the railway. The place was too large and strongly held for the armoured cars alone to take it, but it was intended that if the going was good enough they should be used to cover the advance of the Arabs.

After some deliberation it was decided to move further to the south-east, if possible to Hallat Ammar, the next station south of Mudowarra. Getting back into the cars we started off on the smooth surface at high speed, with nothing before us but the heat haze as far as eye could see. The crew of the 'Grey Knight' were evidently feeling frisky; with a roar they shot past us. This was disheartening, but I had noticed that their driver, anxious to steal a march on us, had changed into top gear almost before his engine had had time to gain a sufficient rate of revolutions. I had roared away in slower stages, so that when ready to slam her into top gear I had full power available. As 'Blast' gained speed we drew level and raced over that billiard-table surface, bonnet and bonnet. Nuri of the piebald steed, thrilled to the marrow, was clinging to the side of the tender in the attitude of a jockey at Newmarket. Lawrence sat carelessly huddled on the seat, but his eyes were tense and eager.

However, 'Blast's' body was slightly longer and heavier than that of the 'Grey Knight,' and the additional load presently began to tell against her. The 'Grey Knight' drew steadily away from us. I glanced at the speedometer; we were doing sixty-five miles an hour. In previous tests I had proved that her best speed was seventy miles, which was not bad for a 1914 Alpine chassis, but that had only been attained when she was entirely unladen. I thought it was hopeless now to attempt to outdistance our opponent. In this I was mistaken, for we still had a reserve. Lawrence - the man was full of the reserve that gives power - had ridden over this flat on his Ghazala, and when you ride or walk you see more than what lies just under your nose. Car-travelling is too fast and busy for close observation of surroundings. 'Steer more to the left,' said Lawrence. I was more than surprised at this, for the 'Grey Knight' was now three hundred yards ahead. The race was lost, but there was no need to disgrace ourselves more than necessary. However, I did as he directed, turning the wheel mechanically and wondering what on earth his object was. There was a gleam of mischief in his eye, but I had not known him long enough to judge how sure his touch might be. The crew of 'Grey Knight' must have thought we were crazy. 'Keep her to it,' said Lawrence.

I was doing my utmost in a dazed sort of way, with my foot hard down on the accelerator and staring most of the time at the 'Grey Knight.' Presently I thought she seemed to slacken speed. She had slackened, and in a few moments we were abreast of her, though separated laterally by a good distance. She appeared to have stopped, in fact; but we had already flashed ahead and I could not be sure. I was amazed at this turning of the tables, and glancing at Lawrence I saw there was a sardonic smile on his face. 'I imagine they have struck a watercourse,' he said, with a chuckle. I raced on until sand-dunes loomed ahead and I had to slow down. We had come to the end of the flat well ahead of the 'Grey Knight.'

We discussed the race at length in camp that night, and we all agreed that the race is not to the swift nor the battle to the strong, but that the man who uses his wits is the one who is most likely to win in both of them.

The new moon set early, and the night was very dark when I walked round the group of sleeping figures during my hour of guard duty. We lay in a slight hollow, where we were protected somewhat from the cold breeze which usually stirs towards morning, and where we stood in less danger of being seen at daylight by prowlers, supposing that we overslept ourselves. We all did a short spell of keeping watch, officers and men, Englishmen and Orientals.

I fingered the trusty automatic which I had acquired in the Senussi desert, and thought of the Turkish railway which snaked along the ground in the darkness somewhere not far ahead of where we lay.

Chapter Fifteen
Blowing Up The Railway

Dawn came at last and we began to stir our cold limbs stiffly. A look-out man was posted on a neighbouring hill to keep watch on the surrounding country while we lit fires and made tea, to drink with our bully beef and biscuits.

Over breakfast the next move was discussed. Lawrence and Zaal naturally had the most to say in reference to our plans, for not long before they had blown up a whole train near Mudowarra. Thirty miles of undulating country still separated us from the ridge from which, with the aid of our glasses, we might see Mudowarra station. The plan decided on was that if no large Turkish patrol was to be seen on that part of the line we would turn southward from there and, keeping behind the ridge which lay parallel with the railway, steal down to a point between Mudowarra and Hallat Ammar, where the railway passed over a two-span bridge, the demolition of which was calculated to cause considerable inconvenience to the enemy.

At last all the details of the operation were arranged and explained. Everybody knew exactly what he had to do, and if anything went wrong we must promptly obey the improvised signals of the leaders. Thus, if Lawrence ran, we were all to run; if Zaal ducked for cover we were all to duck. If we happened to get surrounded by the enemy the cars were to dash off without delay in a given direction, while the rest, still on foot, were to spread out fanwise and make for safe cover, every man to his taste. Later the cars were to pick up all those who were so placed that there was no danger of the vehicles being captured in the course of the operation. All this being arranged, we loaded our weapons afresh, took our seats, and started off as directed by Zaal.

The going was very bad, and our progress slow. Many little ditches had to be crossed and rocky valleys carefully negotiated. It was no light matter to take large cars over these uncharted regions, where even camels find the going rough. However, by noon we came under the last ridge, where we halted. Lawrence got down and climbed stealthily to the top to make observation. He seemed to be absent for hours, and at last, becoming impatient of inaction, I left the car and climbed up by the way he had gone. Just short of the top I found a sheltered ledge and, taking station on this, I peered cautiously over.

With something like a shock I saw the gleaming railway line not more than half a mile away. It lay along an embankment, and about a couple of miles from where I was there stood a square building, towards which the line ran. This was the station of Hallat Ammar. Glancing cautiously to the left I could see Lawrence, now accompanied by Nuri and Zaal, still scanning the landscape. When they caught sight of me, Zaal made hasty signs to me to keep under cover. Afterwards Lawrence explained to me that his previous raid here had been thrown out of gear by Zaal's men exposing themselves to sight on this same ridge, which was in full view of a Turkish observation post; and he recounted the story to me so realistically that more than once I had a creepy feeling in the region of the spine.

Since that raid, in which part of the line had been blown up, together with a train, the rails had been repaired and the railway put in working order as was desired by the Arab commanders, for Lawrence's plan was to keep the large Turkish garrison pinned down in Medina by allowing them to get enough supplies to prevent them marching out in desperation and joining their comrades in Syria, where they would make a most unwelcome addition to Allenby's obstacles.

Through his glasses Lawrence saw that the bridge which he had blown up in the previous raid had been replaced by three heavy wooden trestles fixed in a concrete base. To these had been bolted the steel sleepers on which the new rails were laid. It was necessary to wait till just after the patrol had passed along the line, he said, and then we would dash down and do our deed. We should have several hours, all being well, before the appearance of another patrol. The idea was to make a breach in the line sufficiently extensive to necessitate repairs which would take several weeks, so that Jaafar's army would have time to make their attack on Mudowarra before the Turks were again in a position to send reinforcements to that place by rail from Medina.

At last Lawrence announced that he could see, through his glasses, the patrol advancing up the line, and at once everybody ran to the top of the ridge to take a look at them. Soon they became plain to the naked eye, marching anyhow along the embankment, with their rifles slung over their backs. Lawrence said he thought the stout corporal in charge of them was the very same man whom he had seen on similar duty at the time of the previous raid. They gradually came closer, but it seemed a very long time before they reached the bridge. One would have thought that the sight of the lately repaired structure would have quickened them to alertness, but no, they slouched along disconsolately and without a sign of any interest in their surroundings. They trudged along mechanically, like dejected convicts made to labour for the benefit of their jailer. Their dullness suited our purpose admirably, and it could be safely assumed that the men in the redoubt at Hallat Ammar were hardly more zealous.

As soon as the patrol had passed our position and gone from sight we drove carefully over the ridge and made our way quietly to the shelter of the railway embankment. North and south, everywhere, the silence of the desert was unbroken;

evidently the men in the redoubt had not observed us. Springing out of the cars, we all set to work with feverish haste. Laden with bricks of gun-cotton, I followed Lawrence up the steep embankment. His method was to lay the blocks at intervals flat against the side of the rail, and to fix each one with wire. Finally, a separate fuse and detonator was fitted to every block. Having given us one or two demonstrations of this, Lawrence directed some of us to work along the line to the north and others to the south, our task being to fix as many blocks as possible until a halt was signalled. Lawrence himself worked rapidly, and still found time to make exclamations of satisfaction at every new effort of those who were working near him. We worked on hands and knees, crawling forward after the completion of each block and dropping flat on the ground between the rails at every alarm. Presently, as I moved on in the sweltering heat, I saw some of the smashed carriages which had been blown up in the previous raid and were too badly damaged to be repaired. They lay at the bottom of the embankment in heaps of twisted and broken wood and metal, and some of the woodwork was riddled with bullet holes.

After hours of this work some of us began to get a bit anxious, and to throw doubtful glances towards the Turkish redoubt, which seemed to have grown plainer in the afternoon light. The Turks in there must have been asleep. I was acting as assistant to Lawrence, handing materials and tools to him as he required them. I glanced at him inquiringly. 'Do you think that is enough, sir?' I suggested. I had begun to think he would go on till nightfall, regardless of all risks. He was so wrapped up in the work and completely untroubled about everything else, that he might have been planting flowers in a suburban garden on Saturday afternoon. He paused at my remark and surveyed the work we had done with a look of contentment. Then he looked further along, where the rails were innocent of gun cotton, and I knew by his expression that we had not done yet. He was greedy for more. That is the word - greedy. 'I think we'll go just a little further round the bend,' he said.

'Yes, certainly, sir!' said I briskly. I never in my life felt more anxious to get on with a job and have done with it. We went just a little further round the bend and did quite a lot more gardening. But at last he declared that our work was finished. All the others had ceased their activities long before, and had gone down to the cars. Lawrence walked along eyeing critically all they had done: I followed him. Then he stood still, his eyes still moving along the rails, and thought for some moments. I thought, 'When the devil is this job going to end?'

At last he said softly, 'Run back to the car, Rolls, and get the engine running. Drive back to a safe distance and wait there till I come. Tell the others to do the same.'

I needed no urging, but rushed thankfully down the embankment. I admit this first venture had begun to get on my nerves. I rapped out his message to the others, cranked up 'Blast,' leapt behind the wheel, and drove away to a safe distance, halting parallel to the line, near side on. I looked round for Nuri, but he had gone reconnoitring somewhere, and I could see nothing of him. On the railway line Lawrence was now skipping lightly from block to block of the gun-cotton, with a lighted taper in his hand. With the flame he touched the end of each two-foot fuse in turn. Quickly they were all ignited and he ran down the embankment for cover. I sat waiting for something to happen.

Suddenly there was a loud report, followed by another, and another, as the fuses carried fire to the detonators. Instantly afterwards there was the screaming of ripped iron, as great pieces of the rails were torn clean out and sent flying and whizzing over the desert like shells from a twelve-pounder gun. Then I saw Lawrence running towards me, with his skirts flapping round his bare feet. My nerves were strung to full tension as I sat fidgeting with the gear lever. Then a horrible miracle happened. From out of the sky a heavy piece of rail came whirling at me as though aimed with vicious care at my head. It was about nine inches long, and the inches by which it missed me were fewer. It landed with a sickening crash in Lawrence's vacant seat, cutting a great gash through the flock-filled cushion and burying itself deep in the wood beneath. This was my nearest approach to being beheaded. The missile was of the exact length of a block of gun-cotton, and had been sheared out as though cut by a pair of scissors. Lawrence reached the car a few moments afterwards and his face changed slightly when he saw what had happened: so many escapes were registered by that gash in the cushion which would make his seat uncomfortable for the rest of the trip.

Suddenly we were recalled to the present by the crack of a rifle, and a bullet buried itself in the side of the wooden body. Another near escape! Our friends in the redoubt had wakened, and they now began to snipe us hotly. Nuri ran up shouting that Turks were coming out of Hallat Ammar, and out of Mudowarra as well, as I understood more by his gestures than his words. Lawrence made rapid signals to the 'Grey Knight,' and she began to beat it for all she was worth. I let in my clutch and drove hotly in her tracks. Over the ridge we went and away on the other side, towards the setting sun.

We made our camp that night on the Rumm flat and lit our fires under the rocks. As I passed Lawrence's fire, where he sat with Zaal, Nuri and Joyce, I saw that they were listening enthralled to his Arabic speech. The flickering light lit up their faces in the night, making a curious and unforgettable picture. I have never known a finer story-teller than Lawrence. Years after the war he described himself in a letter to me as a poor correspondent, but added that when he succeeded in paying me his long-promised visit he would be ready to talk for hours.

The next morning we went skimming quietly over the glinting flat, amongst the wonders of Rumm. The single note of the faint song raised by the fast-revolving tires had a simplicity which made it an appropriate sound in those unchanging sunlit streets. Out on the dunes we charged recklessly through the tamarisk bushes until we came on the plain; and so came to the rock of Guweira and the camp of our comrades.

Chapter Sixteen
The Camp Watch-Repairer

During our absence on the raid the men of the armoured car section had learnt more about our Arab allies in their camp massed round the base of the rock. These Arabs were rich compared with us, for each man of them received two pounds a month, and if he brought his own camel he was allowed a further four pounds, but they were not so rich as they wanted to be. Their liberal wages were always paid to them in gold: they would accept no rags of paper. They loved gold so much that they seemed able to detect its presence by the sense of smell. And why not? Iron has a sufficiently distinctive smell, and perhaps gold has too, if one's sense of smell is strong enough. Our chaps had no money at all, as they had received no pay since leaving Egypt. About the only thing there was for us to buy in Arabia was tobacco. This the Arabs had, and very poor stuff it was. Nevertheless, they would take nothing but gold for it; so we turned our attention to making gold in our spare time, when we were not employed in mounting guard over the stack of lead-lined cases, each of which contained five thousand sovereigns for the Arabs.

The Arabs wandered into our camp, flaunting small bags of Turkish tobacco-dust before our craving eyes, for no tobacco of any sort had yet been issued to us in Arabia. Round his lean body, next to his skin, each gold-greedy Arab wore a hollow belt of canvas or leather in which he kept his pelf. This, his private bank, could by no means be forcibly separated from his body while he lived. It was important that our Arabs should live. Lawrence had recently requested us on no account to upset them in any way, as the slightest hostile excitement might

155

easily cause bloodshed, and no one knew where that might end. A quarrel between us and our tobacco-selling allies might ruin months of patient planning and propaganda work amongst them, and with it the revolt itself. If necessary, insults must be borne in patience; pride must be swallowed.

'One guinea!' cried the tobacco-selling Shylocks, holding up their beastly little bags of tobacco-dust.

'What! A guinea for less than an ounce of dust! Get away from here!'

'Very good Tobago,' they would persist, and, indeed, it was more than gold-dust to us, deprived of the means of smoking for months.

This was a problem requiring careful thought. To begin with we were paupers, down-and-outs, for we had received no pay all the time we had been in Arabia. The only way to get that tobacco without resort to forbidden bloodshed was by outwitting the Arabs. A close inspection of all our kit yielded some tarnished French pennies, the relics of our days in the Flanders mud. These had been kept as mementoes; but sentiment is no good without tobacco. Our diligent study of Arab psychology had revealed to us a weakness in him for vain ornaments, an inborn craving to possess cheap jewellery, wrist-watches that told the time in a shout, rings that sparkled like well-polished decanters on a side board, or, failing these, gold, of course; gold in any form.

Months of lonely life in the desert, hundreds of miles from any shop, had sharpened our ingenuity, and the sheer boredom of inactivity of mind and body had led us to fashion small objects out of the most unlikely materials, just as our forerunner, Robinson Crusoe, had done on his island. The cars were our islands, the sand was our sea. Among other things, we had made excellent wedding-rings (perhaps the unconscious expression of another craving) out of ordinary pennies, the lettering and the date remaining intact inside. The outside was carefully filed in bevel form, and polished until it looked very like burnished gold. These rings were, indeed, in appearance, exactly like 9-carat gold wedding-rings, and one of them seemed a fair enough exchange for a small bag of kneaded tobacco-dust. A certain amount of close labour went to their making too. The tobacco was, indeed, valued by its owner at a guinea, but that did not alter the fact that its value in the country which we came from was exactly nothing.

So when the Arabs came offering to sell, they found us ready to succumb to their wiles. In exchange for their miserable bags of tobacco they received fine gold rings. These they gloated over for a few moments and then put on their little fingers – while a faint grin played round their avaricious mouths. The deal was done. We, too, could grin – and smoke. And curiously enough when the gold began to turn black no complaints were heard. Dignity forbade those Arabs from letting their losing simpleness be known, for they were afraid of the scorn of their friends.

One of my comrades thought of another fruitful scheme. When off duty he placed a written notice on the outside of his tent – 'W. R., Camp Watch-repairer' – for the benefit of the Arabs. They could not read it, of course, but they soon noticed it, and also W. R. himself, who sat just within his tent door with an opened watch in his hand, waiting for business. They soon got somebody to interpret that sign to them and W. R. was promptly recognized as a minor wizard. Wedding-rings forgotten, they approached him, holding out their cheap wrist watches, those of them which had stopped. 'Mush kwais,' they muttered, 'not good.' W. R. solemnly beckoned one of them to approach the presence that he might give him succour in his trouble. But first of all he must produce tobacco or saccharine – the sugar-substitute then being issued. This suggestion was not well received. The silent watch must be made to tick first.

No tick, no pay, was the Arab's reasonable suggestion. This he indicated by pointing at his watch and then at W. R.'s tweezers. The terms were acceptable to W. R., who, in his turn, explained by signs and frowns that if payment was not forthcoming when the tick was produced he would, by his marvellous power, mysteriously cause the watch to falter again. As his process was a secret one, he would tactfully suggest that watches be left in his care until the next day, as he had a great deal of work on hand. This suggestion caused very anxious looks indeed, and some proud owners of watches would not consent to it on any account. These W. R. would reassure, telling them that as a special favour he would do the job while they waited. Bidding them to remain outside the tent, he would go in and, dropping the flap, make a rapid inspection of the watch. His little screwdriver would quickly release the balance-wheel; he would shake the watch, blow sharply into it so as to remove the accumulated sand, replace the wheel, and then, with another shake, a ticking would announce that wizardry had done its work. Then W. R.'s voice would be heard by the anxious owner outside: 'Mohammed! Taala hinna! ... Come here, Mohammed!' Mohammed, removing his distrustful eye from the slit in the tent through which he had been trying to keep watch on his property, would skip happily inside. W. R., standing gravely before the tent-pole, would take the watch from out of the air like a conjurer and hold it to the ear of the delighted Mohammed, and payment having been made, the Arab would hasten away with exclamations of delight.

Sometimes, when tobacco was plentiful and W. R. felt in a generous mood, he would mesmerize a batch of silent watches into life free of charge. This was good business, for it created an excellent impression in the Arab camp, and his trade flourished more than ever. He knew nothing of the mechanism of watches, except what he had learnt by picking at the works of those submitted to him, and if his sand-blowing process was at any time unsuccessful he would promptly give the watch a bath in petrol. If even this was of no avail he would solemnly pronounce the death sentence on the watch and hand it back to its mourning owner. It was generally admitted that if W. R. had tried and failed to revive the tick then by no mortal man could it ever be revived.

But with all our schemes we remained paupers, in the midst of hoards of gold, great and small. There was gold everywhere, except in the pockets of the English. We had not a threepenny bit or a piastre to call our own, and only by outwitting the Arabs or by currying favour with them could we get a little tobacco or sugar, the only sweetmeat. Night and day we guarded from the loot loving Arabs the cases of gold which were to be distributed to them alone. At monthly intervals the great day came round when Feisal, sitting in great dignity at an improvised table near the rock, with General Jaafar and the staff in close attendance, made the grand pay out. The men filed past the table, and each halted and stood to attention, with very unusual smartness, in front of his promised king. Frequently the king-maker, Lawrence, was there too, unassuming but not inconspicuous, clothed in white silk and the finest camel-hair cloth, and with the sheen of gold at his head-rope and belt. An officer on Feisal's left would drop two sovereigns in the royal hand, or six if a Bedouin with his own camel was to be paid, and His Highness the Sheriff, with a dignity and a graciousness which few men could have equalled, would hand it over with a word which brought a gleam of pleasure to the man's eyes.

This great day was a holiday for the Hejaz army: all was jubilation and enthusiastic loyalty. The best of the horsemen would career wildly round the rock, flying like the wind on their Arab horses, which leapt like hares and foamed at the mouth. Gathering speed as they came towards the Standard, which stood planted in the ground before Feisal's tent, with cloaks streaming and arms flapping, they would stand high in their stirrups as they came abreast of it, and fire their rifles madly in the air, howling like wild men. And Feisal, sitting on his sumptuous carpet, smiled at them serenely.

Later they would gather in circles round their fires to make coffee and to gloat over their gold, turning the coins this way and that to look at them better, before tucking them away in the money-belts which encircled their lean bodies. Such times had never been known in Arabia, even within the memory of the oldest of them.

Chapter Seventeen
The Watch On Maan

Our more active work now consisted of reconnaissance trips from Guweira, especially northwards towards Maan. Often Lawrence was in camp with us, and then suddenly he would vanish. Today he would unexpectedly make his appearance, mounted on Ghazala, with his bodyguard in attendance; the next day he might signal to a scouting aeroplane from Palestine to land, and in it he would fly to Allenby's headquarters. There were times when we concluded that he would not return to our front at all, when it seemed that we were to be left to swelter in the Arabian heat without a purpose, and with nobody to give us an intelligent hint of what was going on in the enemy's strongholds. Then suddenly a rumour would quicken the listless men. 'The Skipper is back!'

'No! Where?'

'Over there, in Feisal's tent!'

Eyes would turn quickly in the direction indicated, and there, sure enough, we would see Lawrence's bodyguard and a group of kneeling camels. And sooner or later their leader would emerge from the tent. But before long he would vanish from among us again, perhaps in the night, only to reappear as suddenly after the lapse of some days. He was our guiding light; when he was absent we were just so many children in a strange and unknown country, listless, or groping like blind men for something to hold on by. No one but Lawrence seemed to know the reasons that underlay our mysterious movements, or if they did know they never spoke. I often longed for an opportunity to drive with Lawrence again. He was always ready to talk, and if not interrupted he would ramble on for hours, telling of his past doings, and of his plans for the future. I used to stare in wonder when he spoke of such episodes as his attempt to blow up the Yarmuk bridge, while his calm voice went on easily recounting details which almost made one's hair stand on end. Whenever he paused, as though in thought – 'Yes, and then?' I would murmur, impatient to hear the rest of the extraordinary story. And he was prompt to gratify such interest, being always appreciative of a good listener, as well as of anyone who had anything of interest to tell him.

His return was always quite an event, especially in the earlier days, when we were still in almost complete ignorance of our purpose. In the officers' tent there would be a sudden scuffle, as the occupants began hurriedly to smarten themselves up to receive him. This impulse was due to their training, but they grew out of it in time when they had become used to seeing Lawrence come in dishevelled and covered with desert dust, bare footed, and with a ragged Arab cloak hanging anyhow from his shoulders. Yet he had magnificent clothes for pay-days and holidays, or for whenever it was necessary for him to appear in public with Feisal.

Once he came with the armoured cars on a reconnaissance which lasted nearly a week in country of the vilest. As usual, since there were so few of us, the guard duty at night was shared by all ranks. It was well known that we always carried a large quantity of gold, and even the presence of armoured cars might not have prevailed on prowlers to keep away if they thought there was no guard on watch. On one of the last days of the trip the going was so bad that when we camped for the night it was found that there were nine tyres so badly cut that it was necessary to change the wheels. Back aching labour it was too after the long day's driving in the heat, over incredibly rough and rocky country. For my part I was nearly exhausted at the end of it, and I was not the only one. Lawrence had now and then stood watching us at the work, and I dare say the glances we gave him were not of the sweetest. When it was over and done and we had munched a bit of bully and a biscuit and were drawing lots for guard duty with bits of paper in a mess-tin, he came quietly up to the officer in charge of us and tapped him on the shoulder. 'Don't bother about that. I'll do the guard myself. Let the men have a rest,' he said.

'What, all night, sir?' exclaimed the astonished lieutenant.

'Yes, all night,' he replied. 'I must do some hard thinking, and this will be a splendid opportunity.'

There was no need for him to make occasions to get peace and quietness for thinking. More than half his days were spent wandering over the desert with his bodyguard as near or as distant as he chose to order them to march, and there is no solitude like that of the empty desert. And he admitted in after years that sleep was to him one of the greatest of luxuries. His conduct gradually made on our minds an impression that shaped in us such admiration, respect, and affection for him that I believe there was no sacrifice on earth that it was possible for us to understand that we could have refused to make for him, without despising and cursing ourselves all our lives after. I say nothing about the silly sacrifices that are not understood, for these are the soldier's daily contribution to progress; and I do not believe that under Lawrence's direct command such would ever have been called for.

On Lawrence's return from one of his conferences at headquarters we learnt that it had been decided that an offensive was to be opened. Intensive demolition of the railway was to be put in hand, and aeroplanes from Akaba were to keep Maan well bombed. The town was entrenched and protected by redoubts to such an extent that it was well-nigh impregnable, and the garrison consisted of six thousand infantry and a regiment of cavalry. The railway line was our affair, and I believe we did our work pretty thoroughly, keeping four Turkish labour battalions continuously employed in clearing up after us.

Wire-Netting Road At The Commencement Of Negb-El-Shtar.

It was evident that an attack in force on Maan was not far distant, and the next base proposed for our cars was Aba el Lissan, ten miles over the escarpment of the great mountain mass of Shtar, which rose to a height of four thousand feet above the Guweira plain, and could be seen on clear days from the rock. But besides being situated less than twenty miles from Maan, which made great caution necessary in approaching it, Aba el Lissan was cut off from our present camping-place by the difficulties of the ground. Several times we had made reconnaissances towards the place, using great caution not to come within the view of the many Turkish hill top posts which were dotted about. To reach the summit of the Nagb el Shtar was difficult for camels, and by cars the road could only be passed with great labour and patience. Even before the cliff was reached there were considerable difficulties, for a deep belt of sand-dunes stretched in billowy undulations on the plain far to right and left. Wire-netting would have to be carefully pegged down on this soft surface so that our heavy armoured cars might pass over it. When this obstacle had been passed there was the steep face of the cliff to be tackled. The pass was like that at Itm, but very much steeper. It wound here and there in crazy hairpin bends, and the gradients were mostly of one-in-three. Thirteen of such stretches, with a like number of hairpin bends, mounted to the last terrific rise of one-in-two. With every ounce of its power bursting out of the cylinders no car could pull itself to the top of this without a crowd of men straining behind to heave it up with tremendous efforts.

Our first attempt to reconnoitre this precipice with cars was attended with some excitement. We crossed the plain towards the sand-dunes at the foot of Shtar, without, apparently, being observed by the Turks in their stone-built look-out posts, and then proceeded to carefully select a place to cross - for at that time the wire netting, of course, had not yet been laid. It was imperative that we should make as little noise as possible, for sound carried to a great distance in that dry atmosphere. Suddenly my engine began to misfire, and I said to Lawrence, who was riding beside me, that I was afraid we were going to have trouble. He said he sincerely hoped the engine would right itself, as we might have to make a run for safety. I had my own idea about what the trouble was, and thought I could probably rectify it if only we could stop somewhere. My suggestion to this end was not given much encouragement, however, as everybody was intent only on the object of our expedition. I had an unpleasant feeling that the further we went the worse my engine would behave, but I kept my thoughts to myself, and determined to make the car hold out as long as I found it possible to keep her on the move. An inner voice kept on telling me to race the engine, to see whether that would reduce the trouble, but I dare not obey the urge, for fear of exposing our position to the enemy by the noise I should make.

We drew close to the belt of sand-dunes. I knew perfectly well that any attempt to charge it with my engine in this state would get us stuck fast, so I jibbed like a shy camel and stopped dead. My passengers looked at me inquiringly, and I suggested that it would be best if they took cover amongst some rocks close at hand while I tinkered with the obstinate engine, as we could not get much further while it remained in its present state. While the others walked off to a little distance, Tommy, my spare driver, and I dismantled the offending part of the engine. Every now and then Tommy stared hard at the distant cliffs to try to find out whether there were any Turks overlooking our proceedings. At last I straightened my back with a grunt, and announced that I had completed the job. Tommy had gone into a crevice in the rocks, and I followed to ask what he was doing. 'Just leaving my mark,' he said, 'in case we never pass this way again.' I saw that he was scratching a design deeply in the rock face with his knife. 'That's the Staffordshire knot,' he said, 'the emblem of my county.' A curious feeling, like a presentiment of coming trouble, kept me silent. Tommy never saw Staffordshire again. Not long afterwards he was shot by a treacherous Arab, and buried in a quiet grave in great, mysterious Arabia.

The sound of hurrying feet startled us as we stood in the crevice, looking at the Staffordshire knot. The others were returning at the double. I ran out and leapt into the tender, and all the others tumbled in breathlessly after me. That was enough. I knew that a quick exit was desired. I swung her round and made off without waiting for verbal instructions. The air seemed full of a unanimous desire to return post-haste to Guweira. There were Turks in the sand-dunes.

Life in a Rolls-Royce tender in those days was one continuous hustle. I cannot now give an account of all my movements with any attempt at accuracy as to dates. As soon as Lawrence had made up his mind to make any sort of move he put his decision into force instantly. His own diary shows that he was in a different place nearly every day, but this makes no mention of hundreds of trips which lasted only a few hours. At any moment we might suddenly dash off to put a couple of belts of machine-gun bullets into a Turkish repair gang on the railway line, or a message dropped from an aeroplane might send us scurrying out to intercept a hostile patrol. Cars soon became indispensable to the Arab army. At first there had been a prejudice against them, probably because the camel-riding Arabs mistrusted and feared the entry into their country of such a superior and dangerous form of war machine. But before long Feisal began to accompany Lawrence in his rides in my tender, and as all the officers of the Arab regulars were impressed with the advantage of having armoured cars at call, the Bedouins were obliged to make the best of the position.

As the companion of Lawrence and Feisal on many a drive I was in an excellent position to pick up interesting information had I been able to understand Arabic; but as I did not I had to wait for enlightenment until Lawrence rode with me alone, for then he never failed to talk freely.

Once I drove Auda of the Howeitat on a journey. He refused all my pressing requests that he should sit comfortably on the cushioned front seat, and perched himself high on some cases of gold in the body behind. I have no doubt he had smelt the gold, and I am quite sure that such a typical Arab found boxes of gold a far more comforting seat than the downiest of cushions. Such was not my idea of the seat of honour for notabilities; but still it is impossible to sit in a car, at the best of times, with any great air of distinction, and there is no doubt that Aura regarded no seat as honourable to a grown man except the back of a horse or a camel. He had come with us to act as a guide, and he told Lawrence in his deep, guttural tones that he could see better from his perch on the gold. All his life he had lived for raiding and fighting; he was the greatest warrior in all the northern tribes; and now, amused by the unaccustomed motion of car-travelling, he permitted his handsome old face to show a good-humoured smile. When the rear wheels suddenly dropped into a hole and jerked him violently on his perch, he even clapped his hands in juvenile delight and nodded to me as a sign of his approval of my great skill as a driver. There he sat stroking his beard, the man whose single harsh word was enough to raise the hosts of the Howeitat on both sides of the railway line and bring them buzzing in hundreds around the entrenchments of Maan.

And the crews of the armoured cars, bearded and unkempt, sunburnt and ragged, were, in appearance at least, worthy allies of the looting cut-throats of Arabia.

Chapter Eighteen
In Search Of Joy

I mentioned to Lawrence that our fellows were having a thin time, and that if we could get a bottle or two of something for the punch-bowl, and something fit to smoke, it would give a more glorious feeling to the campaign. He smiled, and said, of course, something should be done about it. Later I was 'warned' by the skipper of the armoured car section to drive down to Akaba and report to the captain of a ship which, he said, I would find anchored there. I was to hand the shipmaster a 'signed indent,' and he would forthwith hand me some stores, presumably beer and baccy.

After breakfast Tommy and I shot away in the tender on our errand of mercy, singing like dyspeptic larks to the ragtime snatching of the steering-wheel this way and that as we went between the irregular hummocks. It was a relief when we came to the pass of Itm with its made road, although the surface of this was rough enough. The season was cold and the cliffs of the gorge cut off the biting wind of the upland, which was pleasant.

We intended to draw fresh water from a spring on our way, as we had no wish to drink the chlorinated supplies at Akaba; but as we rounded a bend and came in sight of the place where it was situated, we saw that it was surrounded by a mob of Arabs.

'Well, that means no water for us,' I said, in disgust.

'Oh, does it!' cried Tommy, who was always very contemptuous of our Arab allies. 'We're just as much entitled to it as those black devils.'

'Yes,' I said, 'but can't you see they're armed to the teeth? We don't want to start a shooting match with them.'

I had slowed down so as to see better whether it was of any use for us to try to get water, and as we drew level with the spring and the Arabs around it, Tommy tried to jump out. It was plain to me that though his purpose might be a peaceful one he was fully expecting to meet and repel opposition. An Arab fired at us. With the least possible delay we returned his fire: Tommy with his rifle, I with my automatic pistol. I shouted, 'Keep down, Tommy! They'll get you!' for he was standing up to fire at them.

Crouching low and shooting over my shoulder, I accelerated with a dangerous jerk. Tommy fell down in the car, but immediately struggled to get up again and let fly at the Arabs. However, I intended to take no unnecessary risks, and I raced away from a volley of bullets which lashed the rocks around us. Tommy thereupon accused me of getting the wind up, but I replied that discretion and our orders from Lawrence made a graceful retirement from that mob the better part of valour. We had a slight argument, and he declared that he would look out for an opportunity of passing that way again, by himself. I said, 'All right. Just as you please,' and raced round the bends of Itm without slackening speed more than was absolutely necessary to avoid an accident. As we went by the old Turkish fortified posts, now deserted, we fell silent and showed our ruffled tempers. In a very short time, however, we came to the single marquee which was the base camp of the armoured car section at Akaba.

Sam, the solitary caretaker, who lived like a hermit here in the bed of the Wadi Araba, half a mile from the sea, came out to meet us. He listened to our tale of adventure with a series of grunts, and tactfully soothed Tommy by expressing his willingness to go back with us to the well. A homely, domesticated soul was Sam. He was always glad, rather in the manner of a good wife, to welcome and entertain men who had been wandering in the desert whenever they returned from their wanderings to his lonely home by the sea. Soon he had the kettle boiling on his sputtering primus stove, and while he made tea he inquired after his particular friends in the Armoured Car Battery and cracked the latest Akaba jokes for our amusement.

The tea was excellent, with plenty of milk and sugar, and he had tasty sweet biscuits that you could have eaten without teeth. I asked him how he managed to get hold of these luxuries, but he answered me only with a look. It was an expressive look, suggesting comfortably that we should eat and ask no questions; so the subject was dropped in favour of other topics.

After tea Sam clapped his hands together and instantly an Arab boy appeared from somewhere behind the marquee and proceeded to clear away the few remains of the meal. Sam's enamelled tin mugs all bore his initials, 'S.R.', scratched on the outside. It was evident that while Sam enjoyed the visits of friends from the desert he was under no illusions about their tendency to scrounge anything which might be of use to them in the wilds.

Sam said that the water at Akaba was doctored to such an extent that it was undrinkable, and he himself hired a Bedouin to bring him supplies by camel from the well where we had seen the mob of Arabs. He said he would like to take a trip there himself, as his life held little variety; so we all agreed to go there together in a Ford tender which had been left in his charge temporarily. We put two empty fantassis in the back and prepared to start, Sam assuring us that we should certainly find the well deserted at this hour of the day. 'It was one chance in a thousand that you should have been fired at,' he said. 'I'll bet the sharpshooters have cleared off long before this. Jaafar has preached them sermons about interfering with British troops, and they know that as soon as their doings are reported to him he will scour the desert till he finds them, and shoot 'em without trial.'

Thus comforted, we started in good spirits, laughing like boys at the antics of our Tin Lizzie as she ploughed her way through the sand drifts in the golden sunset light. We soon reached the first of the old Turkish posts, a jutting mass of rock which guarded the approach to the gorge of Itm. Akaba was a centre of fortifications which all faced towards the sea; the Turks had been very thoroughly prepared to repel any landing here. Apparently they had not contemplated anything like Lawrence's sudden assault from the rear, and they had been taken completely by surprise.

We were so engrossed in looking at the spectacular cliffs of the gorge that for some moments we did not notice a curious scene which had come into view further up the pass. A convoy of camel ambulances, conveying sick and wounded, stood there halted, and surrounded by a crowd of Arabs who had evidently held it up. They struggled like a mass of hornets, swarming on the native attendants this way and that. It was clear that a violent wrangle was going on. Suddenly a bullet whistled past my head. I stopped the tender and leapt out of it with a rifle in my hands. 'Take cover!' I shouted as I ran behind a rock. Sam followed my example, but Tommy stood near the car and blazed away with the other rifle. We shouted to him, but he did not or would not hear; so I ran back to him, with the intention of dragging him into the protection of a rock. Before I could reach him he half turned as though intending to take cover of his own accord, but almost at the same moment I saw him whip both his hands to his stomach and collapse on the ground, crying out with pain.

In a moment Sam and I were on our knees beside him. 'Shot in the stomach!' I said to Sam, with vague trouble. It had all happened so unexpectedly. Sam said something, and somehow it became clear to us that we must get him away to where he could receive proper attention. The firing had ceased. Tommy lay there, uttering faint moans, and I expected every second to see him stiffen in death. We lifted him into the Ford, placing him flat on his back, and then we began a slow, horrible journey back to Akaba. There we found our doctor, Marshall, in his tent; and under his direction we carried Tommy into the hospital tent. I believe the doctor operated on him without delay, but Tommy died before the morning dawned. Early on the following day he was buried in the sand, Sam and I and two others carrying him to his grave on a stretcher covered with a Union Jack. A bugler blew the Last Post, and before he had finished the whole valley was shrouded in a whirling sandstorm. Sam and I made a rough wooden cross, which we put up later, and he promised to look after it as long as he remained at Akaba.

My journey alone back to Guweira was not a pleasant one. This, our first casualty, had happened in a manner which would be particularly displeasing to Lawrence, who had repeatedly requested us all to keep clear of quarrels with the Arabs. But the worst was that I had lost far more than a comrade, for Tommy and I had been firm friends. That, too, had begun over our admiration for Lawrence.

In action against the enemy the loss of one man would hardly be noticed, but such a fatality as this might have a serious political effect. Feisal had to order a close investigation of the matter, and eventually six Arabs were sent to Mecca under escort to answer the charge of murder.

At Guweira my news upset everybody, but soldiers on a campaign do not grieve over such happenings; it rather makes them more determined to get the best out of life while it remains to themselves. The grog that night was made pretty stiff, the dixy filled to the brim with liquor. Battered enamelled mugs were dipped in the potent flood, filled, and as they were emptied, passed from hand to hand. For this once, if never before in Arabia, we drank our fill. Then, sprawling on blankets round the wood fire, we sang and sang. The officers, hearing the merry howling, came to join in like stout fellows for once, sick, probably, of their loneliness. The last words, unintelligible, which echoed over the unseen plain were roared to the tune of 'Auld Lang Syne.'

Chapter Nineteen
Camp Moved To Jefer

Our tenders were now kept very busy dashing to Akaba and back again, bringing up stores of all sorts. There was to be an attack by the Arabs under Nuri on Jurf, the second station on the railway north of Maan, and our armoured cars were to assist in it. For this purpose we had to make our advanced base at Jefer, which lay east of the railway and of Maan, and it was decided that we should cross the line between Maan and Ghadir el Haj, the next station to the south. To do this we had first of all to scale the precipice of Shtar.

In two great columns of prancing horses and roaring camels, Nuri left Guweira for his attack on Jurf, and Jaafar and Lawrence left for Tafila. At dawn the next morning our complete Battery moved out on its way to cross the railway. The heavy armoured cars had a great deal of trouble in getting through the deep sand which lay in many places, but with the help of all hands they cleared every obstacle one by one.

Then came the belt of dunes under Shtar. A dash was made for this by the tenders in the heat of the early afternoon. Arrived at the edge, we stopped the cars and hurriedly began to roll out our wire-netting across the sand, making a firm, narrow road for the armoured cars. Eventually they all crossed the sand in safety and came under the high cliffs. It now remained to get up the pass, with its long succession of hairpin bends. How we managed to get every car to the top without attracting the attention of the Turks is a mystery. Perhaps they had all retired to Maan from their outposts. The drivers roared up, with their engines all out, in the endeavour to do the climb without stopping, but the pandemonium did not bring a single Turk on the scene.

The last Ford tender, heavily loaded, very nearly met disaster on the final steep gradient. The driver had steered rather too widely round the last hairpin bend, and his rear wheel very nearly dropped over the precipice. He just missed this, however, and came to rest ten yards up the last incline, as his engine had not enough power to go on. The brakes locked his wheels fast, but on the loose shale of the surface he began to slip back helplessly. Being entirely concerned with checking the backward movement of the car, the driver omitted to alter the steering, and his front wheels remained in the position in which he had turned them when making his narrow escape from the precipice. Everybody rushed forward with stones to place under the wheels, yelling excited and contradictory orders, all of which flustered the driver. Men, straining to hold up the car by sheer strength, slipped and slithered on the ground in clouds of dust. From my position above I could see stones and large pieces of rock hurtling over the edge and falling down the giddy steep. I closed my eyes, waiting for the sickening crash of the car falling after them. Nothing happened, and I opened my eyes again. The struggling helpers were clinging on still, and the car had stopped moving. It had come to rest with its off-side rear wheel hanging over in space and the rear axle resting on the edge.

'Come on, quick!' someone shouted, and several of us who had stood as though petrified at the top left our cars and ran down to help. By the time we arrived the driver had jumped to safety, and by our combined efforts we at last managed to drag the car back on the track. After these strenuous efforts under the dipping sun of the late afternoon we flung ourselves down exhausted, thankful for the chance to rest for a while. From this height – about four thousand feet – the Guweira plain offered a magnificent view, and, lying at the edge of the precipice, the impression on one's mind was of hovering stationary in an aeroplane. The rolling desert-scape was awesome in its spaciousness and its bareness, and was not unlike a golden-brown sea rolling in from the horizon to the base of the cliff on which we lay.

The high plateau to which we had come was of grey granite, relieved by small patches of green scrub; and in place of the yielding sand great rocks lay strewn in all directions. Between these we picked our way carefully, until the stony slopes of Aba el Lissan came in sight. Here we struck a made road in fair condition, descending between steep heights into a valley; and near the bottom of the incline we drew to a halt beside a running stream of clear water.

We got down, and passing by the few rough stone hovels which stood about the stream, we came cautiously to where the road made a sharp turn between two tall rocks, and peered round the bend. We had no desire to encounter a Turkish battalion, which, although we might have beaten it off, would certainly have prevented our secret crossing of the railway. Fortunately, however, there was no sign of man or beast, and we proceeded on our way with the cars in single file, at about fifty yards interval.

Away to the left, in the dusk, we could already see some of the lights of Maan, and hear occasional sounds; but the road now swung to the right, making towards Batra. Silence was imperative, necessitating very careful driving, for the clanging of armoured cars might easily betray our presence and call forth the garrison of Maan. The eerie twilight was fast turning to darkness, a darkness which was necessary to our enterprise, but which added to our risks of accident. However, for my part, I hoped that if we were discovered the Turks would not attack us at night, on account of the difficulty of ascertaining our numbers. They had already learnt to shun blind fighting in these deserts, at one moment empty, the next swarming with

Arabs. Even now, for all the Turks knew, and for all I knew, Feisal's army might be roaming the heights of Batra, or hiding behind its rocks, ready to snipe at the first Turk who showed his bullet head within range. Perhaps if he heard us passing, the Turk would decide to lie low until morning, so as to feel more sure of himself.

Apart from the added danger of fouling one of the projecting rocks which seemed to spring up everywhere, the darkness brought an element of comfort. I was leading the column, and I had a look-out man lying on the front wing whose cries of 'Right!' 'Left!' 'Right!' helped our progress enormously. At the point where we intended to cross the line it passed between the slopes of a sandy depression, and as we drove between the boulders towards this the lights of Maan twinkled at us every now and then, growing brighter as the night closed down.

Suddenly the Arab guide who was with us called a halt, and we came to a standstill on the edge of a slope. The Arab made a guttural remark to an Arabic-speaking officer who was riding beside me, and the latter said in my ear, 'Go very steady. He says we are very close to the line.... Ah! Stop!' The moment he hissed the last words I stopped the car, and we all sprang out, the officer and I gripping our revolvers, the Arab carrying his ornamented rifle. So we crept forward in the uncanny silence. Someone lurched against me and I stumbled and nearly fell. We were treading on a yielding surface, the drifted sand of a shallow valley. I heard the guide murmur, 'Taala hina!' – 'Come this way!' – and as I edged towards the place where his voice sounded from I saw the light of the newly risen moon glistening queerly on something above my head. It was the Turkish telegraph wire which ran beside the railway line, and it hummed softly in the silence. The permanent-way lay just beyond it, half embedded in the drifted sand, and I inspected this with some concern. The last thing we desired was to be stuck on the line itself, in full view of Maan, the lights of which twinkled away to the left even now. Fortunately there was no embankment, and by dropping stones between the rails and on the outer sides to a depth of about six inches we could make a ramp without using wedges of wood. We would then rush each car over and drive into the hills beyond.

Having finished our observations, prepared our plan, and made two crossing-places, we crept back to the others and put all in train for the venture. Speed in crossing was absolutely necessary, for the line could be enfiladed by the machine guns of Maan. If a car struck at the first crossing-place, those following it must turn off and make use of the other. Soon everyone was ready, and I received the order to make the first attempt. I started up the Rolls, with a special feeling of gratitude to her makers for producing such a silent engine. My passengers remained behind, preferring to walk; and setting my teeth I charged forward into the loose sand. She laboured in the heavy going for a few moments, and then as the front wheels crunched on the stones they shot away to either side. But with a violent bump the wheels went over the rail. The rear wheels began to spin, but with a tremendous lurch the car passed both rails and I drove on blindly, gathering speed quickly, until I came to what I judged was a safe distance from the railway. Here I stopped, and jumping out hurried back to help in preparing the track for the next car.

We were favoured by fortune, for every car crossed without much difficulty, and not a shot was fired at us by the enemy. Once mustered on the other side we drove about fifteen miles further, and then stopped and made our camp for the night.

In the cold dawn a thick mist made us hurry to strike our camp and be gone, and soon after the sun had risen we had crossed the twenty miles of firm plain and were come to the camp of the Sheriff Nasir and his Arabs at Jefer. These men looked starved and frozen in the biting wind of the Maan plateau. The cold was intense at times, and there were several falls of snow.

The night before our arrival, Nasir and his men had occupied the ridge commanding the station at Jurf, and had succeeded in cutting the line to the north and to the south. Then the way having been prepared by a few shells from Nuri's field gun, they had swarmed into the station and captured two hundred Turks. They were still full of their success when we joined them at Jefer.

Chapter Twenty
Ambulance Work

Although denied a share in the actual assault on Jurf, we started off the next morning to destroy as much of the railway line and rolling stock in the vicinity as possible, in order to hamper the transport of supplies to the harassed garrison in Maan.

At Jurf we found two engines lying near the station. We placed charges of gun-cotton under these, and also between the points of the sidings and against the water tower and the pump. We ran to the work of destruction, back and forth, blowing up rails and anything else that might be of value to the enemy. We poured petrol on a string of wooden trucks and set fire to them; and so on until there was nothing else left to destroy. Only when the desolation was complete did we feel satisfied - and perhaps a little foolish.

In these hectic days our jobs and loads were widely varied. When not engaged in a demolition raid, driving loaded with explosives to the railway, I might possibly have to carry some proud Sheriff on an important mission, lasting for weeks. Immediately after that I might start off in support of an action in which the armoured cars were engaged. Once two badly wounded men had to be conveyed all the way to Akaba for surgical attention. The deck of my tender was cleared, and the two men were laid in it as gently as possible, under the supervision of Lawrence. 'Do your best to get them to Akaba as quickly as possible, but take the bumps easily,' he whispered to me. The task was an irksome one, but there was never any thought of trying to dodge any job which came from

Lawrence. There was also a curious belief in his star by all of us. I once heard one man say, 'I wouldn't mind going to the moon for Lawrence,' and another reply, 'Yes, and if he gave the order you'd certainly get there.'

So I started off on the two-hundred-miles trek with my crumpled human load. The slightest bump brought cries of pain from the poor wretches, and at every depression I set my teeth as I eased her over as gently as I possibly could. Frequently I was obliged to stop, in order to pack them in a more easy position; then a few more weary miles and stop again, until the strain had begun to tell to such an extent that I felt as though every pain of theirs was tormenting my body too. There was no ambulance orderly to minister to the unfortunate men in their suffering, and all I could do was to drive on with a plodding and grim carefulness, listening for their dreadful groans. It was a nerve-racking experience. Although a Rolls-Royce, free of noise and vibration, she was not sprung in a way suitable for ambulance work, but was meant to carry a ton of anything, from armed men to beef and biscuits. It was impossible, try as I might, to avoid a good deal of jolting.

At last I had covered nearly a hundred miles without encountering a living soul, and had come within shooting distance of the railway line. I had clung closely to the tracks left in the ground by the Battery when we had gone up to Jefer. These would take us to the crossing place, which I knew we could only pass with a series of fearful jolts, and I feared for my wounded on such terrible going, for they seemed nearly dead already. Yet I dared not turn off without more knowledge of the country in the mere hope of finding a smoother path, and so the grim journey proceeded. In any case, I must not delay and fumble in crossing the line, for it was at that point that we ran the greatest risk of encountering a patrol of the enemy.

I was faced with two alternatives: either to take a greater risk of being fired on by crossing in daylight, a risk which included the possibility of capture and death for the two wounded men as well as for me, or to get close to the line and wait for darkness before crossing. For the sake of my helpless passengers I chose the former, and presently I halted beside the last rock which was large enough to give concealment to the car. From there I went forward on foot, bending low as I moved down the rocky slope into the depression. In the soft sand at the bottom I dropped on my hands and knees and crawled up to the line, dropping flat whenever I fancied that I heard a sound. Lying close to the rails, I gathered stones to build a ramp as before, and all the time I heard sounds coming from the direction of Maan. Sometimes I thought I saw the moving figures of troopers, flitting in the haze. The longer I remained there the more nervous I became, and I thought that had I been alone I would have gladly charged over the obstruction and taken all chances of damage to the car; but I had the wounded, and even now I could hear the plaintive voice of one of them crying for water.

I ran back; the man's eyes were rolling as though he was delirious. 'Oh, God!' I thought, 'he is going to die.' I groped desperately for a water-bottle, and having found one, drew the cork out and handed the bottle to him. With a startling effort he clutched my shaking hands with the bottle in them and began to gulp the water. I thought I heard Turks coming towards us, and I tried desperately to free my hands. But he clung on like a drowning man till frenzied thoughts shot into my mind. Should I stun the poor wretch by banging his head against the side of the tender as he drank with my hands imprisoned in his. I could not bring myself to do this to the helpless man, yet how else was I to free myself from his grasp? I was still in a state of uncertainty as to what form of violence would be least dangerous to him when his grip on my hands relaxed and I was obliged to grab him as he fell back unconscious. The water bottle dropped from my hands unheeded.

Meanwhile, the other man had turned his glassy eyes towards us. He said no word, but managed to place a finger somewhere near his lips, and in his eyes there was a look of agonized appeal. He too wanted to drink. But all the water in the fallen bottle was spilt. I was becoming desperate. We must get away from here at all costs.

I sprang into my seat and put her into gear, and we lurched grimly forward. Crash! The front wheels mounted the first rail and dropped on the sleepers. Crash! Over they went again, passing the second rail. I set my teeth for the two jarring bumps of the driving wheels, the crowning agony of a nightmare drive. As the rear wheels struck the first rail the wretched men behind me were thrown up nearly a foot and came down again with a sickening thud. The air seemed full of their squealing cries, and then of their groans. I groaned myself, with mental torture. A Turkish patrol had come into view round some rocks to the southward. We were only just in time. They halted and raised their rifles; there was a crackling of reports, but I pressed down the accelerator and raced up the rocky incline out of the valley, tensely imploring Providence for more speed, and hoping that my tires would stand the strain. I did not stop again until I drew up beside the running spring at Aba el Lissan.

I looked all round the silent place nervously and longed to be speeding on again; but at all costs I must get water for my passengers, or they might not survive the jolting of the next hundred miles. I filled everything I had that would hold water and gave the wounded men each a drink; then I leapt aboard again and shot off into the fading light. When, a little later, we came to descend the face of Shtar, those poor fellows again lived through many minutes of agony. In spite of all my efforts to prevent it, they slithered backwards and forwards with the rolling and pitching of the tender, until I became perfectly convinced that they would not be alive by the time we reached the bottom. When we got there she nearly stuck in the sand, and I dared not think of stopping. With the last gasp of her engine she just managed to reach the wire-netting track, where she slowly began to pick up speed. Once clear of the dunes I raced on in the dusk over the flat to the rock of Guweira.

Here at last I was able to get proper first-aid from Nuri's gunners; but my orders were Akaba, and Akaba I meant to reach. So, after the wounds of my passengers had been dressed and they had been made more comfortable and given something to drink, I started off again in a cloud of dust towards the gorge of Itm. I felt full of confidence and tranquillity now, for although it was quite dark I knew the road too well to go astray.

At last I emerged from the bottom end of the pass which I had helped to make, and saw the twinkling lights of Akaba with a rich feeling of relief. I drew up before the field hospital, and when the orderlies saw my passengers they thought at first that they were dead. They were covered with the desert dust, so that their faces were like the faces of ghosts, and the blankets which covered them resembled white shrouds. I, too, was smothered from head to foot in the white dust, and as soon as the tender had been relieved of its load I lost no time in going in search of food, and quarters for the night.

Next morning I reported to Colonel Joyce for further orders, and by him I was detailed to return to Lawrence with a supply of money. This I transported to Guweira - a sum of £30,000 - where it was to await our leader's arrival.

Chapter Twenty-One
The Battery In Action

As soon as Lawrence appeared in sight of the camp at Guweira, Nuri's cavalry galloped to meet him, racing one another and firing their rifles excitedly in the air. On coming up with him they careered round him in wide circles, whooping their delight. It was curious that these Arabs, generally so suspicious of strangers, should become so devoted to an Englishman. By nature they are hero-worshippers, but I doubt whether so many of them have ever before made a hero of one of an alien race and religion. His power over all was so unquestionable that there were times when I felt that he was not just one of us, but that there was something different about him, that he was in some way superhuman. He threw himself so completely into his great task that his words and acts seemed to have a prophetic quality, and to so impress all who came under his influence that they were moved to follow him, and so to unite in a common cause. It is said that he distributed half a million pounds in gold to the Arabs. To that statement should be added another, and that is that for all we know to the contrary it is plain that anybody else who had distributed it would have done so in vain.

Often I saw Lawrence rapidly entering notes in a pocket-book, and once when we were driving together I asked him what it was he was writing. Questions never gave him offence, and he answered me without any hesitation that he intended to write an account of the campaign when it was all over, as a record for himself and for his friends who had worked with him. His wish was to give each of them a copy of it as a gift, and this he intended to do if he could afford the expense. 'But surely you will publish it, sir?' I said in astonishment.

'I hope I shall not be forced to do that,' was his quiet answer.

Here was further proof of his self-denial, and, as is well known, he only published the abridged version of his book in order to pay the debts which he had incurred in the production of the magnificent copies which were presented to his friends.

Lawrence did not remain with us long, but was gone in a day, mounted on the cream-coloured Wodheiha, one of the finest racing camels in northern Arabia. With him he took the bulk of the £30,000 which we had brought up from Akaba, having distributed it among the loads of his bodyguard. This money was to enable the Sheriff Zeid to continue his operations at Tafileh, near the southern end of the Dead Sea.

In Palestine Allenby was now preparing to smash his way through to Damascus, and it had been decided between him and Lawrence that the Arabs should take Maan and then advance to the north, keeping pace with the British Desert Mounted Corps. While Jaafar's Arab regulars were assaulting Maan the Armoured Car Battery was to move south to Shahm, Ramleh, and Mudowarra, which places they were to capture. The railway line was then to be destroyed at intervals all the way from Mudowarra to Maan, so that there would be no further danger of the garrison at the latter place being reinforced from Medina.

The Arab army, equipped with a train of two thousand fresh baggage-camels, and well supplied with ammunition and all kinds of stores, which had arrived from Egypt, became exceedingly proud of themselves. The increasingly lofty attitude of the Arabs towards the British details who were employed with them plainly showed that we were only tolerated on sufferance, for the sake of pleasing Feisal and Lawrence, not for any real value we might have as soldiers. I remarked on this to Lawrence on one occasion, and after listening to what I had to say he reminded me that every dog has his day, and recommended me to wait in patience for mine. There was not much satisfaction in this, but there was nothing else to be done.

As is well known, Allenby's offensive of April 1918 failed, being repulsed before Es Salt, after his troops had crossed the Jordan with some difficulty, and fought their way that far. The news reached the Arab leaders while the attack on Maan was still in progress. That place was found to be well-nigh impregnable, and by the time the attack had begun to weaken, Jemal Pasha, following up his success against Allenby at Es Salt, sent a heavily escorted caravan of ammunition and supplies into Maan, the railway to the north having been put out of action by the Arabs.

In the meantime our armoured cars still lay at Guweira. The many conflicting rumours which reached us had made us all so sceptical that any newcomer who came in with 'news' was promptly classed as a liar, and told to report to the doctor for medical treatment. Some of these newsmongers reported that the new commander, Colonel Dawnay, had brought into the desert all the scientific methods of Whitehall. This we refused to believe, until one night a startling order reached us. The guard was to polish its buttons. This was duly done, and when the guard paraded the sergeant in charge read out in full the duties required of a sentry, just as is done in a well-conducted barracks.

Lawrence arrived suddenly by car, like the wind in the night, with other stragglers from Maan. The failure of his plans did not outwardly disturb him, and he still kept his assured and pleasant smile. At the first opportunity I asked him about our fortunes. There had certainly been a temporary setback in the two most important parts of the strategic plan - the attacks on Es Salt and Maan; but success at Mudowarra, which he seemed to consider certain, would do a lot towards restoring the balance. The Arabs still had the upper hand in their zone, and it was practically impossible for them to lose the initiative.

On the morning after his arrival all the Ford transport was loaded with the necessary supplies; while the Rolls-Royce tenders were equipped with the usual raiding gear, machine gun and ammunition, gun-cotton, battery, exploder, and a supply of gold.

Next day, after breakfast, my car, in which I carried Lawrence and Colonel Dawnay, led the column from Guweira in grand style, the armoured cars following at regular intervals, with their guns all turned forwards at exactly the same angle, without any variation. The procession must have been very impressive to a spectator, had there been one. This was the first time that Lawrence's guerrilla tactics had been attempted with such a force, though in this case we were under the command of Dawnay, who had prepared an elaborate scheme of action based on the best models. Lawrence was with us as interpreter and liaison officer with the Arabs. His hit-and-run methods would not have suited Dawnay, though with them the required result was usually obtained with much greater economy. Besides Egyptian Camel Corps, Bedouins, a mountain-gun battery and the armoured cars, there were aeroplanes for bombing, which were to operate from the Rumm flat.

Our first objective was the station of Shahm, the third southward from Maan. The pace set for the heavy column was an easy one, but the dust rose in choking clouds from under the wheels of the cars. For a short time the column maintained its ordered line, with cars separated by regular intervals, but presently they began to turn aside in order to avoid the dust of those in front, and also to choose better places for crossing stretches of loose sand. The safest method was found to be for each car to pick its own course, and in any case the thick dust soon made it impossible to see ahead.

As we approached Rumm I began to put on speed, for I already had experience of the treacherous dunes which bordered the flat. Soon we were in the thick of these. The drivers of the following cars imitated my example, charging through the sand with a roar of the exhaust, and finally we ran through the last tufts of tamarisk, and glided smoothly down the lofty street of Rumm. Here was a parade ground fit for a general review; so on this, the first halt, we drew up our cars dressed by the left in true military style. There had been some speed rivalry on the way, and as soon as we stopped, the various drivers began to discuss the different performances of their cars. The two Canadians, nicknamed Skip and Gink, were famous for their wisecracks, and their voices were soon heard above the rest. 'Waal, Gink! I guess I passed your crazy lawn-mower.'

'You wait a bit, Skip,' retorts Gink. 'If you've never seen a real fire-engine, just you watch this guy shoot across that flat. Those tires will get so hot that they'll throw out fireworks.'

Then Skip, 'Oah yeah! Why, this automobile will shoot past that baked-potato can of yours so that you'll think your sparks have let loose a rocket.'

Groups of officers and men stood about discussing the chances of the raid. The drivers of the armoured cars imagined themselves charging with a grand swoop on the station, with their guns spitting death at the enemy. Most of the officers were engaged in studying maps and discussing Colonel Dawnay's elaborate plan. Lawrence went apart and paced round the parked cars in a wide circle, with his head bowed and his hands clasped together in front, a favourite attitude of his when deep in thought. He was clothed in his richest robes, with gold headrope and dagger, and his long face was half hidden by the silken folds of his kefiya.

Soon the order came to march. All the engines began to sing merrily, and the crew of each car mounted to their places.

Then, while I waited with my car for the two chiefs, who were watching the scene, they all moved off, leaving only the faintest trace of wheels on the natural concrete of the dry swamp. They set their course like ships at sea, and went sailing away into that wide space where there were no longer any obstructions to be seen. As they advanced they spread out in line abreast, and the spinning wheels were lost in the gleaming light reflected from that smooth surface. So they ran swiftly away, gliding into the haze like grey torpedoes; and every one of them was clearly doing its utmost to outpace all the rest.

Lawrence and Dawnay mounted to their seats and I let in my clutch and flew after the racing Battery. Soon we were in the thick of the race, and keeping pace with them we were able to observe their antics. A Rolls-Royce armoured car drew ahead, passing a fussy little Ford tender loaded with all sorts of gear. Then a Rolls-Royce tender came to the fore, screaming past us at nearly seventy miles an hour. Having shown the mettle of his car the driver slowed her a little, so as to give somebody else a chance of tasting glory. Lawrence pointed out to me another Ford which was straining to get to the fore, panting visibly. For some distance it skimmed along, bonnet and bonnet, with a great Rolls-Royce armoured car, its driver obviously putting every grain of power into the effort. For a few moments it seemed that he would pass the armoured car, then, very suddenly, there was a loud report and the Ford whirled round like a firework on a stick, turning two complete circles and narrowly missing the armoured car; then it rolled over in a double somersault, throwing off its load in all directions. I turned my wheel and drove straight to the scene, fearing for the fate of the driver. The Ford was standing squarely and quietly on all four wheels, as though it had just been pulled up to allow the driver to look for his cigarettes, or something equally simple. Only the driver was ruefully rubbing a bump on his forehead, but even the bump was a very slight one. This driver was afterwards nicknamed Lucky Archie.

Up till this time there had been no speed limit imposed on car drivers in the desert; the desert, in most places, limited speed much too strictly for all concerned. But after this flat-racing episode an order was issued and solemnly read out to us to the effect that cars would be restricted to a certain speed limit - I forget what it was - in order that the wear and tear on government property might be kept down as much as possible. In other words, speeding was made a 'crime,' except, presumably, for armoured cars in action.

In camp that night, above Shahm, the mechanized section of the army was drawn up in an imposing mass. The armoured cars were arranged in a single squadron, dressed by the left, and all with their guns pointing forward at exactly the same angle. Behind these the three Rolls-Royce tenders were drawn up in line as a supporting unit, for, as said, they each carried a machine gun. Then came the ten-pounder guns, mounted on Talbot cars, and lastly the transport, mainly consisting of Ford tenders. The Turks had never shown Arabia anything like this.

Sentries mounted guard at various and numerous points, with orders to continue pacing smartly backwards and forwards, meeting one another in solemn silence at the end of their beat. The rifle of each of them was to be slapped smartly on the butt when a junior officer approached, and was to be 'presented' to anyone over the rank of captain.

At properly spaced intervals machine guns were placed ready on their tripods, with belts inserted, and ammunition-boxes placed at hand. The Arabian Night was turned into an Aldershot Night, and only the enemy failed to do his part. Lawrence walked amongst all this, beaming with delight; but I noticed that Dawnay, the wizard who was responsible for it, showed neither pleasure nor displeasure.

Every move had been worked out to the last detail beforehand, and if every bullet had not been detailed formally to its particular billet before it was fired, at least it is true that the time at which Shahm station was to fall into our hands was stated in orders to the exact minute. Actually, I believe, it was taken a few minutes earlier, but whether this breach of orders amounted to mutiny or not, in the view of our commander, I did not hear.

Long before dawn the various motor units moved to the positions which had been assigned to them as supports of the Arabs and the Egyptian Camel Corps. Two of the three Rolls-Royce cars had been detailed for railway demolition work, but mine was to act as staff tender, a sort of grand-stand for Dawnay and Lawrence.

As the dawn came into the sky the scheme began to work, and we three sat in my car watching it from a hill-top. Dawnay, with an open map on his knees and his watch in his hand, checked every movement of each part of the force as it fell due, to make sure that all were working strictly in accordance with his time-table. Exactly on time the armoured cars swarmed over the top of the ridge behind which they had been concealed, and rolled down towards the first of the Turkish entrenchments. Almost at the same moment the mob of Arabs rushed from behind their hill. Hazaa, their leader, possessed no watch, and would have been unable to tell the time by a watch had he had one. He was a weak link in the chain of our uniformity, and so he had been told to follow the armoured cars in their assaults on the various posts. The other two tenders had already been driven close to the railway line, and their crews were preparing to demolish three bridges. The Egyptian Camel Corps, too, were on the move to time, though the men were obviously gun-shy. The machine guns of the armoured cars were crackling merrily, and the ten-pounders on the Talbots were splitting the air with deafening bangs. Now a couple of aeroplanes flew over from Rumm, which they were using as a temporary base, and dropped a few bombs on the station.

I received orders to drive here, to dash over there, this way, that way, so that Dawnay could see that his scheme was going right at every point, or could put it right if it seemed likely to go wrong. Sometimes we would stop for a few moments to enable the commander to use his field-glasses; then off again over the rough ground in a hectic rush. Once we drove down to the railway to help in the demolition. By midday we had covered over fifty miles, merely in dodging for short distances hither and thither. Once when we halted for a few moments I asked Lawrence what he thought of our prospects. He was watching the scrimmage round the station, and he replied with a mischievous smile that we seemed to be snatching the victory, but not quite in the right way, for our fellows were taking the station now, and it was only twenty minutes past eleven. The station had been ordered to fall into our hands at eleven-thirty; but still, perhaps the fault could be shifted on to the Turks. They were walking out of the building at eleven-twenty, with their arms held up in the classical attitude of surrender.

This was our cue. My engine was purring gently, and the moment I received the order I charged down into the thick of the scramble. In the pandemonium the Arabs were fighting together for the loot and screaming like tigers, some on camels, some on foot, some trying to make off with plunder, others still searching for it. Lawrence and I were first into the office, and he took the station bell as a souvenir, while I took the rubber stamp. The Turks looked on in fear of the Arabs, who were half mad with the lust of loot, and were rushing blindly hither and thither. In the midst of the howling din one of the Turkish mines exploded in the station yard, a camel having trodden on its trigger. The Arabs and the Egyptians began to quarrel about the loot, each claiming the first pick, and shooting began amongst them. Lawrence managed to stop this, and then the Egyptians were allowed to take what they wanted. Finally, on the word 'Go!' the Arabs moved in like a solid mass of ejected inmates from Bedlam, determined to get back within walls again if it cost them their lives. The walls of the station storeroom caved out under the force of their pressure, and the whole place collapsed on them. They went on looting amongst the stones and mortar and dust, and so well were they satisfied with their fortune that three-quarters of them cleared out into the desert, to return to the encampments of their tribes, laden with plunder and glory.

Our next objective was Ramleh, the station south of Shahm, and one armoured car was now sent down to it so as to ascertain its strength. The gunner sent a burst of fire through the station window, but there was nobody there. As soon as this state of affairs had been reported the Arabs tore away down the line to Ramleh, where the rest of them gorged themselves with loot, and cleared off, like their friends. That was the end of the Arabs so far as this expedition was concerned.

The rest of the day was spent in doing damage to the railway line. The other two tenders were quickly at the first bridge above Ramleh, and with Lawrence I now dashed over some terrible going to join them. I was still a hundred yards away from them when the crews sprang up and waved their arms frantically, warning me to keep away. I stopped the car quickly and looked inquiringly first at Lawrence and then back to the others. But they had disappeared again under cover, and before either of us had said a word there was a blinding flash in front of us, followed by a thunderous roar. The shock of the explosion nearly lifted us out of our seats. Stones, sand, and pieces of iron rail shot up into the sky, and we fell together instinctively in an effort to find protection from the coming hail of iron and rubble. It came before we had found any proper protection, and half buried us where we sat. I am not sure who had the worst of the shower, but something hit me a heavy bang on the shoulder, and Lawrence came out of it covered from head to foot with white dust. However, we kicked our way clear of the debris and then went to join the others in their work of destruction.

In the centre piers of most of the bridges there was a small drainage hole, just the right size to allow two bricks of gun-cotton to be fitted in tightly; and the explosion of these, so placed, did more damage than a much greater quantity of explosive would do if stacked on the ground under the arch. The two blocks placed in the hole usually carried away the whole of the arch, and it was therefore the cheapest and most effective method. We set to work to blow up all the bridges and culverts we could come at. Dawnay's scheme was in abeyance, and all the troops, English, Egyptian, and those few who remained of the Arabs, gathered round us to watch our activities. Among these activities was the planting of tulips, an invention of Lawrence's, that thoughtful gardener. In the earlier days we had destroyed lengths of the line by fixing one slab of gun cotton to the side of a rail. But the usual effect of this was merely to shear a short piece of rail clean out and send it flying across the desert like a shell. The Turks could easily repair such damage by simply unscrewing a few nuts and slipping in a new rail. It was in order to make repairs more difficult that Lawrence began to think out another method of making his quick demolitions.

This line was laid on metal sleepers, which could be transported easily and in a comparatively small space, and which were simple to lay. They were set in the loose sand or gravel, and the rails were then bolted to the iron chairs. Lawrence's latest method of making the line unworkable was to push a single block of gun cotton underneath the centre of a sleeper. This could be done without tools, as it was only necessary to scrape away with the hand a little of the sand on which the sleeper was laid. The effect when the explosion occurred was to lift the sleeper up in the middle, and the springing of this tulip drew the rails together, so that they were forced out of the parallel position for over thirty yards. This damage was difficult to repair in a hurry.

Shouts of delight came from the onlookers as we hurried up and down the line planting tulips. Lawrence went nimbly from sleeper to sleeper, manuring them with a lighted taper, the skirts of his cloak flapping about his feet. As soon as one section of the line was worked out we leapt into the tender and drove nearer to Mudowarra, covered by the machine guns of the armoured cars, the drivers of which took care to keep them beyond the range of flying stones. On and on we went, until miles and miles of the line had been twisted out of shape, and its bridges lay in ruins. The sport became irksome after a time, but it was our fault if we had made sport out of our work. This was the grim work of war, and it had to go on, whether we liked it or whether we grew sick of it. Perhaps we were destroying a railway to help in the creation of an empire; perhaps, like sheep, we were merely going where we were driven; but, at any rate, most of us had had more than enough by the time the order came to stop.

The final and the most important part of Dawnay's scheme was the attack on Mudowarra, and in camp that night there was some doubt as to our chance of an easy success, since we no longer had the help of the Arabs. But there was a strong hope that the garrison would be found to have fled, like that of Ramleh. It was a hope that was not realized.

The fatigue and excitement of the day were not followed by a night of ease, for not only was our strict military order and discipline maintained, but the guard was doubled as a precaution against a surprise counter-attack. I went on guard at midnight and spent a detestable two hours in pacing monotonously back and forth near the sleeping figures of the others, lying like dead bodies on the ground. The cars lay parked behind a ridge, and my beat extended from them across a depression to another ridge. The distance was about thirty yards, and by daylight the railway line was in full view all the way. So I paced to and fro, while the time dragged wearily on, with no sound except the snoring of a sleeper, and no light anywhere to be seen. I felt I would have welcomed a surprise attack by the enemy: anything to break the horrible monotony.

I noticed that each time I passed Lawrence's silent figure, stretched on the ground like the rest, he seemed to stir restlessly. I was right; and after I had taken a few more turns he got up and began to pace with me. As a matter of fact, it was the continually returning scraping and crunching of my boots on the stones which had prevented him from sleeping, but I had to obey my orders, even though, as he then told me, the row I made would have given away our position to anyone within a mile of us in that silent desert. Wakefulness and peace, he declared, was far better than the hectic nightmare of tramping feet passing a few feet from your head. He was soon talking of other things, and his remarks were so interesting and amusing that my spell of duty was over in no time. But I continued walking up and down with him long after my relief had taken over the sentry duty, very much to the latter's astonishment. I should have liked to have gone on listening to Lawrence's conversation until dawn. He himself remained on his feet for the rest of the night. But unlike him, whose wakefulness only seemed to increase his power of concentration on the next day, I had an urgent need of sleep to enable me to keep my wits about me when awake. I crept away and stretched myself comfortably across the front seat of the tender, and not until I received a violent shake by the sentry at the first streak of dawn did I realize that all the rest were up and busy. The whole camp was alive with dark figures, moving this way and that in the mist.

After drinking a cup of tea we moved off through the gap between the ridges, and came out on the flinty plain. Presently we came in sight of Mudowarra, and with the aid of glasses a train could be seen standing in the station there. A few moments later there were flashes in the pale mist that hung about the place, and then the howling and roar of bursting shells. The shells, though they fell somewhat short, were well aimed, and we made off without delay, circling away to a long bridge further north, which was out of range of their guns. This was the place where, some months before, I had come near to being beheaded by a flying piece of rail torn out by a slab of our gun-cotton. This time we blew up the bridge very thoroughly, and then we moved north again towards Ramleh, and destroyed more of the line. That day the desert seemed full of the flashes of explosions, and the smoke and dust of shattered bridges. Bridge after bridge, and mile after mile of the permanent-way were destroyed, so that the whole line between Maan and Mudowarra was in ruins, a distance of eighty miles, and Maan was separated permanently from Medina, the headquarters of the Turkish forces in the Hedjaz. We were now more free to give direct help to the British Army in Palestine.

Chapter Twenty-Two
Dinner With Feisal

Our successes about Maan had made our base at Guweira obsolete, and it was decided that we should move north to Aba el Lissan. This would not only bring us within easy striking distance of the chief Turkish stronghold in these parts, but it would remove the awkward necessity of having to pass the terrific Shtar precipice whenever we wanted to make a raid in that direction.

The summer heat had now come in earnest, and almost before the morning mists had vanished the sun struck at us savagely. Feisal had already established his camp at Aba el Lissan, and soon the day came for our remove. Pitching and swaying in the choking dust, the cars left the rock behind them and bumped their way towards the distant cliff. Some of the drivers chose the old tracks which had been made in the sand on our former expeditions, while others preferred to try virgin ground. The heat inside the armoured cars must have been infernal, but discomfort was forgotten in the heartening knowledge that this move was the long awaited sign that our fortunes had at last taken a decided turn for the better. Indeed, it was the beginning of the continual use of the armoured cars in the desert campaign.

Shortly after our arrival at Aba el Lissan I was detailed to go to Akaba on an urgent mission. My orders were to start early and to make the double trip of about two hundred miles in one day - not a light undertaking in the heat of the Arabian summer. I made Akaba in good time, and left again on the return journey without being delayed. But by the time I had climbed to the last rise of Shtar darkness fell. This was unfortunate, for we had only about five miles to go. The safest proceeding would have been to camp where we were until the morning, for the Maan plateau was strewn with large stones and boulders, but as I was anxious to keep to my orders to get back to Aba el Lissan the same day, I decided to go on at slow speed, with a look-out man lying on the front wing to help in picking a safe passage. Laborious work it was. First he shouted, 'Right!' then 'Left!' then 'Right!' again; while I wrenched the wheel this way and that in accordance with his directions. Suddenly he shouted 'Stop!' in a voice that would have brought the Seven Sleepers to their feet with a jerk. I seized and tugged at the brake-lever, and at the same time stood on the brake-pedal; but it was too late. There was a shocking crash, and the car stopped. 'What is it?' I shouted to the look-out man. 'Only a stone,' said he, in a reassuring tone. I got out and looked to see what had happened. 'Only a stone!' I cried. The front dumb-iron had struck a huge boulder, not a loose one, but a fixed outcrop, and was badly bent; and the front axle had been forced back and put out of shape too.

This was serious, but I decided to try to crawl the remaining distance to camp. Then followed what seemed hours of bumping and lurching as we proceeded slowly over the uneven ground. At last a Cockney voice cried in the darkness, 'Halt! Who goes there?'

'Nobody,' said I, 'only us and the donkey-barrow. And we're not going; we're coming.'

'Gawd!' said he. "Ow the dickens did you git 'ere ?'

'Oh,' says I, 'we came by the High Street.'

'Parse, friend! All swell,' said he.

We parsed friend all swell, but the worst was yet to come. My misdeed, or rather its effect, was noted with inward joy by a peevish N.C.O., and eagerly reported by him to higher authority. I found myself a prisoner under open arrest, charged with driving without due care and consideration, and with causing wilful damage to Government property. My case would be brought to the notice of the acting Commanding Officer, and in the meantime my trusty car was to be handed over to the care of somebody else. My immediate explanations were not accepted.

The next day I received a visit from the acting Commanding Officer, who had been informed by that zealous N.C.O. that my car was a complete wreck and would probably have to be sent to England for repair. The acting C.O. told me this, and I could not repress a smile. He looked kindly at me, however, and I asked him whether he himself had examined that mass of wreckage – which I had driven five miles in the dark last night. He said he had not examined it, but the report of the N.C.O., an expert, alleged carelessness against me, and he was afraid it would mean serious trouble for me. Had I anything to say? Oh, that 'Have you anything to say?' Of course, I had a lot to say, if that was of any use; but the irrelevancy of all this palaver was beginning to get on my nerves. I faced him squarely and said, 'Sir, if you will give me two men to help me I will have that car back with the rest in as good condition as it ever was in five hours from now.'

He just stared at me with wide eyes, as though I had taken leave of my senses. However, he came to after a few minutes and said, somewhat dubiously, but not unsympathetically, 'Very well! Carry on! Pick which men you like, and good luck to you.'

It was neck or nothing. I must succeed, or be forever disgraced; but with the skill I possessed, and given a little luck, I had no real doubt about the issue. I knew very well what I was talking about, although here in the desert, far away from any workshop, it did seem a bit of a gamble. I began to scheme intently. If only I could get the necessary degree of heat the job would be enormously simplified. In the cook-house there were two big blow-lamps which were used in our high-speed cookery. These I borrowed by squaring the native cook. The two helpers I had chosen could be relied upon to do their work in quick time and with understanding. Without delay we drew a tarpaulin over and round the car, to give us some protection from the heat, and to keep off intruders. The stage was now set, and we three were stripped to the waist, ready for our part. The time was just two p.m. I whispered, 'Come on, lads! Now for it!'

It was a real race against time, and the hardest job I ever tackled; but that car stood in the rank by seven p.m., straight and dead true, the damaged parts nicely painted to match the rest. We had completed the job on time. Later the Commanding Officer came sauntering round. At the sight of my car he stared in amazement at its transformation. Then he held out his hand to shake mine, and said, 'Well done! I think I understand what happened.'

However, I did not escape without punishment, for I was presented with a stripe for this achievement, and so had my small freedom still further reduced. Lawrence sympathized with me when I told him about it a few days later.

We had not, in fact, been settled many days at Aba el Lissan when Lawrence arrived there on a visit to Feisal, and then at last we were given more news of what lay in store for us. Allenby had given the Arabs two thousand camels to enable them to join efficiently in his coming advance towards Damascus. The Arab headquarters were soon to be moved to Jefer, first of all, and then further to the north; and we were to go with them. In the meantime, Maan, which would cost too much to take, was to be reduced to a proper state of impotence.

Henceforth there was little rest for the armoured cars, and still less for the tenders. The Turks in Maan were permanently besieged, to all intents and purposes; and one day our intelligence service received the news that the garrison intended to make a sortie, or perhaps a dash to get clear away to Syria. On the other hand, there was information that a large number of Turkish troops had been concentrated at Amman for the purpose of relieving Maan. To help in coping with both these menaces the Sheriff Zeid, with half the Arab army, was stationed at Waheida, to the north of Aba el Lissan, where he could reinforce Nuri, who was further north, at Hesa, or attack the garrison of Maan, as occasion demanded. It was not long before word came to us that the sortie was about to be made, and while Nuri led his troops down from the north we prepared to attack from the south-west. We started off to an advanced camp in Wadi Musa, which was the best route for us to approach Maan. According to the plan of action, we had to wait here until aeroplanes from Akaba had gone ahead to bomb and reconnoitre the town. We heard their droning at about nine o'clock on the morning following our arrival in Wadi Musa, and soon they came in sight. There were three of them, and they were flying very low, as though they had difficulty in maintaining height with their heavy loads of bombs. As soon as they had passed ahead of us we made our way forward, between the huge boulders on the southern bank of the stony valley. In front the aeroplanes looked as though they must surely hit some of the great rock pinnacles which towered everywhere. We were still pushing our way forward, twisting and turning this way and that, when the roar of the falling bombs smote our ears, and soon afterwards we could see the aeroplanes turning in circles as they sought for targets. The puffs of smoke from anti-aircraft shells floated in the sky all about them, and as they flew between these they made a fine sight.

A few minutes later we heard the reports of Nuri's ten-pounder guns, and as we had now come on to high ground overlooking Maan we could see the shell-bursts. This was our signal for action. Ammunition belts were quickly slipped into the breeches of the machine guns, and a stream of bullets whistled musically across the valley and ricochetted on the iron roofs of the engine sheds of Maan to the accompaniment of the tat-tat-tat-tat of the guns. Smoke and fire seemed to rise everywhere in the town, and the noise was infernal. Our guns were fired in relays to prevent them all boiling together: as soon as one batch ceased fire another opened up, so that the shower of lead was continuous.

Hedjaz Troops Leaving Akaba.

An aeroplane dropped a message - 'Enemy troops moving north, up the line.' It must be the task of the armoured cars to head off this party and scatter them. The order was given, and the cars immediately turned to the left and began picking their way among the stones in the bottom of the valley, making for the opposite side. They got across without mishap and then set their course for the north-east so as to intercept the enemy a few miles north of the town. The drivers, already well experienced in the art of stone-dodging, swerved from side to side, the cars swaying and pitching like small boats in a rough sea. It was a fine exhibition of trick driving.

Soon they caught sight of the Turkish infantry, and the gunners, sitting knee-deep in a tangled mass of empty belts and loose cartridge-cases, opened fire on them, while the drivers each made towards what seemed to them to be the best targets. The Turks appeared to be taken by surprise, perhaps not imagining that armoured cars could move so fast in such rough country. However, they scattered over the desert and continued on their way northward until brought to bay or shot down by the gunners in the cars.

Meanwhile, we in the tenders drove on to Maan to see whether it was necessary to blow up anything with our gun-cotton. The Arabs had already arrived there, of course, and the excitement of looting was so intense that it seemed impossible that they could sort themselves out without bloodshed. They snatched and tore, ripped and cut everything they could lay their hands on, yelling like fiends in a frenzy of mad desire for possession. We left them to it and turned towards the engine sheds. None of these had a whole roof, all being torn and smashed by shells and bombs and riddled by our machine-gun bullets. Several engines and wagons stood on the lines, and the place contained large stores of rails, sleepers, and trestles for repairing wrecked bridges. There were machine shops fitted with the latest German machinery for the repair of locomotives and rolling stock, and containing tier above tier of labelled bins, filled with every conceivable kind of spare engine part. Such a modern and well-equipped depot in the heart of the desert astonished us. It was no wonder that the enemy had held the place in force, and strained every nerve to repel all attacks on it. Yet now they seemed to have abandoned it.

The armoured cars presently came in, the men in them weary and stained with battle, but very proud of their achievements. 'Well, we've routed the enemy,' said one. 'Smashed them up completely,' said another. Their cars stood anyhow, just pulled up here and there in disorder, like market carts; and the men, having got out of them, had flung themselves down on the ground anyhow, to rest after the excitement and the victory. They did not even bother to make a tour of Maan, but told one another that this was an amusement that could be indulged in at any time.

Suddenly we heard a faint droning in the air to the north-west. 'Aeroplanes!' I exclaimed, but nobody cared whether they were aeroplanes or Zeppelins. The noise grew louder and louder; and then somebody blurted out, 'I'll bet they're enemy.'

'Rats!' retorted another.

'By Jove, he's right!' somebody shouted. 'There's three of them making straight for us!'

'Yes,' I cried, 'and I can see black crosses under the wings.'

'What !' they shouted, jumping up all together in alarm.

There was a sudden shout, 'Look out! Take cover!'

Then they were upon us. I could see the faces of the observers staring over the side, and their features looked terrible with a lust of hatred. I ran to an armoured car, with the object of crawling under it; others did the same: but the pilots dived low, they seemed to be almost on our heads. I could have sworn that one of them had chosen me alone as his target. I fell flat on my face. Some of the others seemed to be still running about. The bombs were tearing great holes in the ground. There were stray camels and men running about. Then the bombs fell further away. The pilots had gone over the town, and the looting Arabs were running wildly into the desert, scattering in all directions.

Presently there was a curious silence, broken only by a faint droning. The aeroplanes were flying away. We lost no time in driving away from the dangerous vicinity of the town, and before morning the place was re-occupied by the Turks, whose main body had been driven back by Nuri's men.

Back at Aba el Lissan, we continued patrol duties to the eastward, so that the receding tail end of our column flitting across the railway line must have become a familiar sight to the Maan garrison. Except for an occasional rifle shot they now took no notice of us.

Then, suddenly, the order came that we were to move to Jefer. We had not seen Lawrence for some time, so nobody knew what the purpose of this new move might be. With many of us, dislike of the Arabs grew stronger as time went on, and it was with difficulty that we could make a show of acknowledging their officers as superiors.

These feelings against the rat-witted men and their comfortless, wretched country were particularly venomous when we had to get up in the misty darkness before dawn; but we were always soothed by the happy news that we were to move to a new camp, for there was always a dim chance, added to our hope, that it might be a British one.

We passed over the railway and struck out on our old track to the north-east, floundering as ever in the yielding dunes. By noon we reached the edge of the great Jefer mud-flat. The heat was intense, and the perspiration poured from us, soaking our shirts as fast as they tended to dry in the hot atmosphere. When our shirts did dry they set hard as wooden boards and chafed the skin to rawness. There was no water to wash clothes in the desert in summer.

This plain glinted before us with crystals of salt. For twenty miles it was as level as a billiard table, and here, unknown and untried, lay the finest speed-track it would be possible to find, with a surface as firm as fine concrete. Our cars glided gaily on the smooth ground, and presently we drew up on it for the midday halt. Tarpaulins were hastily rigged between every two cars, as a protection for the men from the pitiless fire of the sun. But the flies we could not shut out; they settled on us in swarms, and all our savage swishing at them was of no avail.

At last the call to action brought a hope of relief, and soon the purring of the Rolls-Royce engines announced that the armoured cars were ready and waiting to begin the last dash over the plain. Then, as each driver was listening attentively to his engine to assure himself that the cylinders were firing evenly, a sudden barbarous rattle arose in the hot air as the Tin Lizzies were started up. An order was called out, cut-outs were opened, and to the note of a deep roar the armoured cars shot away into the dancing heat haze. We in the three Rolls-Royce tenders waited behind, as was our custom, for these were the times when our differences were to be settled. It was the constant aim of each driver to doctor his engine so that he might claim for it the distinction of being the fastest in the Battery, and we were all in the habit of trying every known trick, and of inventing new ones, to this end.

As soon as the armoured cars had got well out of sight, one and another of us shouted 'Go!' and away we flew, skimming like bees over the flat. In a very few minutes we were racing along, at reduced speed, among the armoured cars and Tin Lizzies, the drivers calling out, 'All present, sergeant!' or some other announcement of their arrival. 'Good!' says the sergeant in his grimmest voice. 'You'll be for guard tonight.' There is loud laughter from all the steel chariots and the column proceeds.

The Emir Feisal and the old sheikh of the Rualla tribe, Nuri Shaalan, were met together at Jefer, and as we drew close to that place we could see the shack-like tents of Shaalan's followers dotted about on the plain. Soon a number of horsemen galloped out to meet us, and with these keeping pace on either side of the Battery we moved slowly into the camp.

We had hardly settled in our station there when a faint droning was heard in the sky. All stared in the direction from which it came, and as it grew louder a speck became visible in the blue. We hastened to roll out the strips of white calico which, when properly placed, formed a huge letter T - our signal to aircraft that the spot was safe for landing. As the aeroplane drew nearer we could see the British circular device on the underside of the wings. Two heads could be seen over the side of the fuselage. 'It's the Skipper!' said somebody. 'The Skipper, for certain!' said another. 'Aurans! Aurans!' came in sudden guttural exclamations from the Arabs. The machine made a sweeping turn and then sailed down to make a graceful landing.

We rushed forward, the Arabs rushed forward, everybody seemed to hasten to greet the man who, without any official announcement from first to last, was recognized by all as the moving spirit of the whole campaign. He had flown from Guweira.

It will not be easy for anyone to understand just how we feel about Lawrence unless they are able to imagine themselves in our place. Even so, it will not be easy for those who have never known the man. For months we have been marooned in the desert, a place populous enough, it seems, but inhabited only by men whom we instinctively mistrust and dislike, whose language we do not understand and whose customs seem beastlike to us. We hate the Arabs. Turkish prisoners, with their sense of order, with their European uniforms and their understanding of military discipline, are like dear friends to us compared with our Arab allies. Here we are, living cheek by jowl with these fierce looking fellows whom we loathe, and with whom we can never get into touch. It is far worse than if the desert had been empty of all but ourselves. For months this goes on, so that the feeling in us grows and grows that we would do almost anything to get away from these savages, who watch us continually and seem all the time to be thinking of nothing but how they may loot our baggage and gear. And then Lawrence comes quietly into the camp, and at once the difficulty has vanished, the riddle is solved. We rush forward: we will carry him shoulder-high, as heroes are greeted in our country. The Arabs rush forward, touch his knee with reverent hands, kiss his shoulder, his head. Damn the Arabs; there must be some good in them after all! But they seem to claim him, as though he belonged more to them than to us. What shall we do now? For the moment we stand quiet, watching with all our eyes. Lawrence knows what is best to do. He gives us a smile of greeting, and we feel in it a touch of regret that he has to conform first of all to Arab custom. Well, he is quite right; this is the Arabs' country: so be it. Instead of swinging him up on our shoulders we watch while Feisal advances through the lane cleared in the mob by his black slaves to meet him. There is a smile on the ivory bearded face. They clasp hands, and quickly the Arabian prince embraces our Lawrence, once, twice: perhaps he kisses him on each cheek; I cannot see. I feel embarrassed at the sight, but it does not last more than a moment, with Lawrence there to set the pace.

There is now a visible link between us and the Arabs. We do not like them more than before, but we feel for them a sort of respect. There is also a visible link between us and our own British Army, between us and England, between us and home. There is more even than this; for now we feel gay with the warm assurance of a purpose, a purpose in which we shall succeed.

That night Feisal invited us all to eat in company with him and some of the greatest sheikhs of the desert. At the appointed time we assembled in his great tent, rather shyly, for even our own notions of table manners were largely disregarded in those days, and in this company we feared to make a complete exhibition of our ignorance. I myself had feasted only once before in Eastern fashion – on that memorable occasion in the beautiful garden of the Siwa Oasis when we were the guests of the sheikh of the district. However, Lawrence's presence soon allayed our fears, and completely altered our view of the whole proceeding. He was the chief guest and sat at Feisal's right hand, the centre of interest to all the nomad sheikhs. I never saw any other of our countrymen - and among the officers who came to us from the Arab Bureau at Cairo there were several experts in the Arabic language and in all matters relating to the Arabs - command any sign of enthusiasm in the least resembling that which was accorded to Lawrence as a matter of course, every time he appeared among them. He now seemed to be serenely at home while he and Feisal chatted happily together, each gnawing a bone or swallowing a fistful of rice between their remarks. Frequently Feisal glanced across at the men of the Armoured Car Battery, and every time he did so he clapped his hands vigorously, as a signal to the slaves to pay closer attention to our needs. With Lawrence sitting there, honoured and supremely at ease, we began to have almost a warm feeling for the Arabs, and I believe they felt the same towards us; and expanding in our pleasure we gorged and gorged until our faces glistened with the effect of our exertions and the fat of the tender mutton.

At length we were sated, and then we moved to the coffee fire, round which carpets had also been laid for us to sit on. While we were drinking little cups of their bitter coffee, a messenger rode in with news. Saluting Feisal, he handed him a dispatch, and Feisal passed it to Lawrence, who scanned it quickly. He spoke to Feisal, and then told us that Colonel Buxton, with the Imperial Camel Corps, had taken Mudowarra, the station which had twice formerly been unsuccessfully assaulted by the Arabs.

Chapter Twenty-Three
At The Well

A few days after Feisal's dinner-party Buxton with his British camel corps arrived at Jefer. Having been told by Lawrence that their plan was to come on here, we had lain about waiting for them and turning our eyes continually in the direction from which they would come, when somebody cried out, 'I can see them!' At once we all stared out across the great Jefer plain, shading our eyes with our hands. It was like looking out on a sea, with every little wave reflecting back into our eyes the flashing light of the sun. In one direction the mirage created a beautiful ornamental lake, edged with castles and tall palm trees which were reflected in its water. And then, across the surface of the lake, we saw a moving string of what appeared to be swans. They were swimming steadily and their long, webbed feet could be seen dangling under water. It was a very curious illusion, and some time elapsed before we saw that they were Buxton's camel-riders. Then, while they continued to crawl, more like ants than swans, over the immense plain, two Tin Lizzies were cranked up and whipped out with some of our men to take our first greetings to them. One of these brought Buxton back, and he was shown into Feisal's tent. Soon the whole force rode in, delighted to see us, as we were to see them.

However, sentiment must not be allowed to get the upper hand on active service, and foreseeing that all those men and camels would require a great deal of water, which it would take them a long time to get out of our well, I came to the conclusion that it would be wise for us to get our supplies before they began. I gave the word, and quickly some of our fellows ran up with empty fantassis and placed them in the body of my tender. Then taking Sanderson, my spare driver, and two others with me I drove without delay to the well. Our spirits were damped before we reached the water, for as we approached I saw that the place was swarming with Arab tribesmen, struggling and disputing over the filling of their waterskins. Our chance looked hopeless, and we sat in the car about fifty yards away wondering what was best to be done. Presently I said, 'Come on! Lend a hand! It's no use waiting here.'

We all got down and, each pair of us carrying a fantassi, we sauntered casually right into the middle of the yelling mob, wearing an air of blissful ignorance and whistling a tune. The last part of our effort to divert their attention was of no use, for even with the aid of a megaphone no whistling could have been heard above that pandemonium. However, everybody was too busy with his own affairs to pay much attention to us, so we edged our way, with an air of unconcern, towards the well and, in spite of scowls, managed to reach it. We had already half filled one of the tanks with our canvas bucket before they realized that they, who never yielded to anything but force, had let themselves be over reached without a struggle. Then things began to look unhealthy, but by making mystifying signs I managed to pacify or bewilder those who were nearest to us. Our progress was terribly slow, however, and I breathed a sigh of relief as each bucketful of water was poured into the tanks. I had no cigarettes or anything else to bribe the Arabs with, and so I had to hold the mob back by sheer force.

Soon the pressure from the rear became overwhelming; my back felt as though it would break in the effort to prevent us and the water tanks from being pushed helplessly into the well. I was certain that the language of the Arabs was terribly profane, and I was thankful to be spared the additional burden of understanding it. Presently violence began amongst the nearest of the mob. One Arab leapt like a tiger on the shoulders of another next to me, and a free fight began. I promptly dropped on my hands and knees and began to crawl between the thicket of brown legs, dragging the half-filled tank after me. The others extricated themselves more quickly than I did, so they came to my aid, and at last we were able to hurry back to the car in triumph.

So far we only had one tank and a half of water. 'Let's get just one more,' I said; and after a little hesitation we returned to the fray. Between us we had produced a little tobacco dust, and when I had moistened this into a pulpy mass I managed to roll a cigarette with it. As we advanced I held this prize up so that all could see it. The effect was remarkable, many skirted warriors running up to me, crying 'Backsheeshi' and in a few moments even those about the well's mouth, hearing the cries of the others, ran back and began elbowing their way towards us. 'Slip off, you two, and fill up while we work the oracle!' I said to two of the others; and when they had gone I began a long palaver with the Arabs so as to delay their return to the well as long as possible. At last I handed the cigarette to a burly rascal, and then I proceeded to search in my clothes for more. This demonstration held the interest of the mob until, on seeing our fellows staggering towards the tender with their tank full of water, I gave it up with a gesture of regret.

But as we all came close to the car again we saw that a grinning crowd there were helping themselves to water from the other fantassis. We immediately broke into a run, shouting 'Yalla! Imshi! Clearout!' All the Arabs jumped off the tender, with the exception of two lanky youths. These continued to stand there defiantly, and they were in the act of upsetting the remainder of the water for the amusement of the crowd when we ran up. I leapt fiercely into the body of the tender and faced the two wretches and ordered them to clear off at once. One of them got down, but the other stood there sullenly till I advanced towards him, when he backed away. I believe I gave him a push when he delayed to jump down, and he shot over the side in a heap amongst the grinning spectators. That indignity took away his self command. His face, when it appeared a moment later over the side of the tender, was like that of a ferocious wild animal. He whipped out his dagger and was back in the car in a flash. There was now to be trouble, the last thing we desired; but self-defence came first. My automatic was in my hand, and I should have used it, but before I could do so our fellows had flung themselves on the Arab and dumped him out of the car.

The crowd was no longer merry, and it was necessary that we should get away from that place without delay. But in order to drive away somebody must get into the driving seat, and the driving seat was already closely besieged by the mob. I suddenly thought of a tin of bully beef which I had in the tender. Taking this out of the box in which it lay, I held it aloft for the crowd to see. At once they all lost interest in everything else and, moving my arm deliberately back so as to let them see what I intended to do, I threw the tin of meat as far from the car as I could. With a howl the crowd rushed after it; and at once Sanderson slipped into the driving seat, started the engine, and drove off as hard as he could go towards our camp, while I clung to the side with the others, in a mood of contrition for allowing myself to violate Lawrence's most important orders.

As we arrived back in camp Buxton's camels were just starting out to the water. 'They've got my sympathy!' said somebody. 'Yes,' I said, 'they've beaten the Turks; now let's see how they get on with their allies.' I did not see any more of them, but a rumour went round later that there had been a dispute at the well between them and the Arabs, and that one of the Camel Corps was captured or abducted and held to ransom, Lawrence paying a handsome bribe in order to procure his release and smooth the matter over.

On the following day Lawrence and Colonel Joyce took my tender as a staff car. When these two chiefs of the Arab revolt were together their conversation went on endlessly, and the miles slipped away happily for me in listening to their remarks, which were full of interest. I did not pull up until we reached Bair, a vast camping ground with two wells.

Chapter Twenty-Four
Azrak

At Bair, where Buxton's Camel Corps were to make their next camp, we picked up a young Bedouin as guide, and then drove on to survey the ground at Azrak, the proposed northern base for the Arab army. The guide sat with Sanderson, my relief driver, commonly called Sandy, perched on top of the spare petrol, gun-cotton, and boxes of money, while Lawrence and Joyce sat on the front seat with me. The armoured car which had accompanied us from Jefer was ordered to continue the journey with us.

Despite her full load, my car roared grandly over the flinty plain, and the snort of her exhaust echoed away in the distant hills. I noted with a cynical interest the looks of serene contentment and satisfaction on the faces of my two companions on the front seat. They lay back at their ease with the air of having read in some infallible time-table the information that at half-past so-and-so tomorrow evening they would arrive at their destination without having to think any more about it. I had not their confidence, and I felt, though probably I was wrong, that they had exaggerated notions concerning the powers of the car in getting over rough country. The miles sped by quickly enough, but only I knew how patchy the going was. I continually had to move the lever from one gear to another; from top gear down to first, then up again by stages. The roaring of the engine filled the air every other minute as I worked the accelerator, and only occasionally was there a spell of quiet, when we came to smooth, hard going. But I was mistaken about one of my companions at least, for presently, after a few quiet words of encouragement,

Lawrence began to speak about the car, and I found that he had even counted the number of gear-changes that I had made since starting from Bair!

At one point we ran into a herd of grazing camels, and the armed herdsmen broke off their singing to run up to the cars and point out to us the position of some thieves who, they said, were lurking ahead. We turned that way to look for them, and chased them for a mile or two, when they stopped and made their camels kneel. When Lawrence had lectured them they went off back by the way they had come.

After passing the hills known as the Three Sisters we came to a number of small watercourses with deep sand in their bottom, and were obliged to collect and lay scrub bushes in a track across them before venturing the cars. In some places the wheels sank into the sand, and we had to use our poles in order to move. All helped in these tasks, and arduous work it was; but at last the sun went down and we made our camp for the night.

Next day in the cool dawn we were soon skimming over the shallow depressions which shelved down to the great Wadi Sirhan, at the northern end of which lay Azrak, the place of our destination. But not until the middle of the next day did we come on the wide flat which lay before the marshes there. The heat here was intense. It rose from the mud flat in shimmering waves which almost stopped our breathing. In the distance I saw tall, pointed reeds, or it might have been a mirage. Almost gasping for breath, I pressed the accelerator hard down and flew in the direction indicated by Lawrence. For a few minutes the wind created by our speed gave a little relief, but soon I was obliged to slow down again as we came to the opposite side of the flat, and then the heat seemed to increase a hundredfold. I had to apply the brakes rather suddenly as we came to a wavy surface of damp mud. Here we left the armoured car under the cover of the marsh reeds while we skirted the treacherous patches of ground and rushed through some low dunes where tamarisk grew, coming out on firm ground beyond.

Climbing up a slope dotted with graves marked by rough stones, we looked over the top and saw great pools of water lying in the hot stillness, but there was not a living soul to be seen. I drove close by a smaller pool, and round an area of black lava, and so came on another flat, across which the ruined castle of Azrak stood up gaunt in the sunlight. As we approached this abode of ancient Arab kings its grim walls seemed to frown upon us, as though disapproving of anything so modern as a motor car.

I pulled up close under the walls and, getting down, followed Lawrence and Joyce into the ruin. They went up the tower, while I remained below. But presently Lawrence came down alone and began wandering about the lower part. He beckoned me to go to him and, pointing to what looked like the crumbled mouth of an old well, bade me look into it. It appeared to lead into a sort of cellar, but all was black down there, and I could see nothing. I looked at him inquiringly. He said to me, 'Once I was kept a prisoner in that dungeon for months.' I was amazed to hear this, but there was more to come yet. He leaned down and pointed to the inside of the hole, at a place where the light just reached, and said, 'Do you see those scratchings?' I looked, and saw something which appeared as though the decaying surface of the stone had been recently scraped away. I looked at him again without speaking. 'Those are some of my attempts to escape,' he said.

He went out of the ruined hall and I followed, wondering as I went whether the full tale of his adventures would ever be told. Getting into the car again, we returned to where we had left the armoured car and followed by it, we returned on our tracks to Bair.

Chapter Twenty-Five
Back To Aba El Lissan

At Bair we found the rest of our Battery, and also the British Camel Corps and a mob of Arabs. The wells were besieged by a struggling crowd, but our armoured car men had drawn their water and were reclining at their ease in circles round their fires. Sanderson and I began to tell our news, but we had hardly commenced when the noise of heated wrangling broke out amongst the excited crowd at the wells. Apparently Lawrence's haughty bodyguard had fallen foul of the rest, and yells of pain and hatred announced that punishment was being meted out to some of them with no gentle hand. The brawl delighted us British soldiers, of course, and we got up to have a better view as it was growing dusk, hoping that some really amusing entertainment was about to be presented for our benefit.

The excitement grew and grew with every passing moment; the scrimmage became more violent; the curses and the groans more hair-raising. But suddenly it all went out like a snuffed candle. A small figure had appeared in the midst of them as if by magic, and the effect was marvellous. The men of the bodyguard desisted, all desisted, and a sort of shamed hush fell upon them all as Lawrence moved amongst them. They looked at one another as though hardly knowing themselves why they had so suddenly stopped their wrangling.

As for Lawrence, he had an errand ready for some of his bodyguard, and having chosen those he wanted he sent them away on their camels. As always, we were amazed to see his uncanny power over these brigands, whose everyday sport was robbery with violence.

Long before dawn Bair was roaring with the din of the various units, breaking camp. The cursing voices of Buxton's Englishmen, struggling with their accoutrements, was mixed with the deep guttural sounds of the Arabs and the neighing of restive Arab horses, and a deep, steady note underlying all was made by the groaning of thousands of camels. Metallic notes were added by the rattling of rifles and the clanging of fantassis.

The armoured cars were to remain at Bair while Lawrence rode with the Camel Corps for a raid on the railway; but it was impossible to sleep any longer in that uproar, so I got up to see them all move out at dawn. As the first daylight came into the sky the low, distant hills which hid the camping ground on three sides came into view, and the great column of riders and transport camels could be seen stretching for miles, until its head was lost in the distance.

Subsequently the raid on the railway had to be abandoned, owing to the unexpected presence in the vicinity of large numbers of Turks, and about a week later the Camel Corps returned to Bair by way of Azrak. Lawrence came with them, and the Armoured Car Battery received the order to return to Aba el Lissan. We set out, Lawrence riding in my car as usual, and as we knew the way well by this time we were able to indulge him in his love of speed to the top of his bent. With his face screwed up and reddened by the rushing wind he sat huddled in his Arab clothes while we careered over the sandy flats, I doing my utmost to keep the lead of the rest, who were trying to pass ahead of me. Now and then a burst tyre in this or that car would put a temporary stop to our antics, and then Lawrence would watch us with an amused smile while we strained and sweated at the task of changing the wheel. Often when a car stopped the others passed it at speed, with the occupants waving their hands to the driver and shouting jeering farewells, but at some time or other a halt had to be called to see whether we were all more or less present, and somebody sent back to look for the missing.

Over the Jefer flat we flew at sixty miles an hour. An armoured car was running alongside, racing my tender bonnet and bonnet, and I pushed her to the limit of her power. 'Sixty-three!' shouted Lawrence - you had to shout if you wanted to be heard, for we had no wind screen - and then, 'Sixty-five!' Still I kept the accelerator hard down, trying to get the last ounce of power out of her. Lawrence glanced back, and then shouted, 'Here comes another tender! He'll overtake us!' 'Righto!' I shouted, and glancing at my speedometer I saw that we were doing sixty-seven.

Suddenly there was a violent scream of escaping air, the car swerved away to the right in a crazy curve, and something went rolling ahead on the course we had been taking. It was one of my back tires which had come off and was continuing the race by itself. This mishap delayed us for some time, but it was all in the game, and although such troubles might have been avoided to some extent by cautious driving, nobody ever let slip a chance of relaxation for such a reason. Every officer and man revelled in these speed trials, and all were ready to help each other to put right the little troubles which were sometimes caused by them.

When the scattered cars had gathered again we made tea and sat in a circle on the sand to drink it, with Lawrence beaming round on the unkempt band as they indulged in back-chat one with another. On this occasion the chief subject was beards: whose beard was the longest and thickest. We all had beards, for no one had shaved since we had left Akaba, and some had not even washed. In fact, I believe that in this gathering Lawrence was the only clean-shaven one present.

After the brief halt we headed straight for the point below Maan, where we intended to cross the broken railway. We passed this without seeing any sign of the enemy and were soon afterwards in sight of Aba el Lissan, whose cool spring and granite rocks were a great relief to our eyes, half blinded by the yellow- sunlit flats of the desert. Lawrence immediately went to confer with the officers of the staff about the coming move against Deraa, the great railway junction south of Damascus. It was intended that the Arab army should cut the Turkish railway communications at this point just before Allenby began his new offensive on the Jaffa Jerusalem front.

The peace of Aba el Lissan was broken rudely by the troops which were passing through it on their way to Azrak, accompanied by their supply columns. From our elevated camp we had a fine view of the huge camel convoys strung out across the dusty plain below, as they came from the rock of Guweira towards the Shtar pass, by which they were to ascend to the plateau. One day, as we were watching this sight, a green motor car made its appearance in the throng of camels and began to climb the pass. It was Feisal's own Vauxhall. But soon it came to a stop on the steep gradient, and we saw that it was in difficulty, so a number of us hastened down to lend a hand in getting it up.

We met the 'Green Linnet,' as we called it, standing and steaming about half-way up the pass. It was still boiling and hissing when we arrived, and Feisal himself, standing beside it, was directing that large stones should be placed behind the wheels to prevent it from returning to the plain below. An anxious crowd stood around the vehicle, which had become a sort of mascot for the Arab army, talking and making gestures at it. When we began to man-handle it their anxiety increased, for they seemed to be afraid that we might spoil the beautiful green paint, and if it had been studded with diamonds they could hardly have watched us more closely. Having sized up the sentimental circumstances, we pushed the 'Green Linnet' up the pass with all the solemnity we could muster, and reverently trundled it on to the Maan plateau, where no more impertinent precipices waited to check its proud course.

A few days later the armoured cars were ordered north again, and in my tender I carried Lawrence, Sheriff Nasir, and Lord Winterton. As the two Englishmen had to sit in the front seat with me, I had to adjust my load so as to form a suitable seat on it for the noble Arab in his splendid robes. However, when I had arranged a seat with the gun-cotton boxes and a petrol case, first removing several projecting nails from them, he nodded and smiled his satisfaction, and settled down to enjoy the trip, while Lawrence looked on approvingly from his front seat. We duly started, and every time Nasir was shot upwards to come crashing down again in a dishevelled heap on the hard wood I thought he would complain of the rough accommodation we had given him. But he made no complaint, and always when Lawrence glanced back and inquired about his welfare he forced a smile to appear on his tortured face, and replied, 'Good!'

Lawrence and Winterton discussed car-travelling in the desert as compared with camel-riding, and seemed to prefer the latter, which was not only less bruising, but also gave better opportunities for sleeping on the march. But when we came to the Jefer flat, and there shot away more smoothly and swiftly than an electric train, they ceased to talk of camels.

At Bair we heard news that the Turks were about to reinforce Maan, but this would serve our purpose splendidly, so long as they did not reinforce Deraa. On the following afternoon we reached Azrak once more, and here I decided to replace several damaged tyres, do some adjustments to my engine, and then bathe in the pool in the cool of the evening, when I hoped the bloodthirstiness of the mosquitoes and flies would have been sated on the bodies of those who bathed earlier. I had just finished the tyres when somebody tapped me on the shoulder, and I glanced round to find Lawrence standing behind me with a thoughtful look on his face. 'Yes, sir!' said I.

'Will you go back to Aba el Lissan and return here without

delay with all the gold you can carry,' he said. 'Can you find your way without a guide?' 'Yes, sir,' I said, 'I've travelled the road several times.' He told me to take my own and another tender, with a spare driver for each, to drive all out by day, and camp at night, and not to get too far to the west in case I was seen from the railway. 'Good luck,' he said. 'Don't be taken prisoner; I'm relying on you for that gold.'

I had to forgo my bathe, and I hastened to round up the other three unfortunates. They received their orders without enthusiasm, but there was no time for them to give vent to their objections, and the cars - all of which were kept in readiness to move off at a moment's notice throughout the campaign - were promptly started up. The troops looked at us with perplexity as we moved out and drove away to the south by the way we had come; but we were quickly out of sight of the camp, and by sunset had covered a hundred miles. We now drew the two cars up side by side, turning their bonnets away from the night wind and covering them with tarpaulins so as to keep out the heavy dew which made them difficult to start in the early morning.

We had intended to fill up the petrol tanks and make all ready for the morning before ourselves settling down for the night, but we had driven a little too long, and the darkness had stolen a march on us. It was dangerous to show lights in the desert, but one of the party found a stump of candle and, having covered himself, his petrol tin and the tank of his car with a tarpaulin so as to hide its light, he began to fill his tank by its flickering flame.

In the meantime I had cleared the space of ground between the cars from stones, and I then began to shake out the blankets, while the others were busied in opening tins of bully beef. Suddenly, as I was energetically shaking a blanket I was very nearly blown to the ground by a terrific 'Woof!' or muffled explosion, and great flames shot into the air from the open petrol tank of the other car. I stood as though mesmerized, while rapid thoughts shot through my mind that the cars would be burnt to a cinder in a few moments, leaving us on the open desert miles from human aid. Suddenly I came to active life again. 'For God's sake, come on!' I shouted, and we all ran to my car and pushed it with all our might until it was some distance from 'Blue Mist,' the car which was now belching flames. Leaving the others to push it further away I whipped up the blankets and, running to the other car, clapped them on the flaming tank, and so held them until the fire was extinguished and there was no longer any danger.

I felt terribly guilty, as, although the foolish act had been that of 'Blue Mist's' driver, I was responsible for the discharge of our mission, including the safe arrival of the cars at Azrak at the end of it. I had seen the driver at his dangerous game and had failed to warn him against it, partly through thoughtlessness and partly because our system was to have everything ready overnight for our start in the morning. When we were really assured that all was well with the car we joined hands and performed a wild dance under the stars.

The car which had been endangered was an older one than the others, which were of the latest Alpine type. By reason of her age and the weakness of her back axle she was used as a spare tender, and she was capable of a good turn of speed. She was reputed to have been the finest motor car of her day, but by the time she came to us her beautiful sporting body had been exchanged for a small box-body suitable to her new employment. The single rear wheels with which she was fitted had handicapped her for desert work, so we had given her double wheels. But these had proved too heavy for her, causing her to lag behind the Battery pathetically in fast treks; so we had been obliged to fit single wheels to her again.

After this incident I lay awake for some time, wondering whether the Turks had seen the fireworks we had treated the desert to, and picturing to myself what I should do if they made an attack on us. I reviewed this and similar matters backwards and forwards for a long time; and then it suddenly occurred to me to ask myself what Lawrence would do in such a case as mine. I decided that he would probably roll over and go to sleep, and my faith in him was now such that within a couple of minutes of this thought coming into my head I rolled over and went to sleep.

At dawn we rose bright and lively, hungry for food and more miles. We ate a hasty breakfast and then at the first swing of their crank handles both engines started beautifully. We roared them up once or twice and then moved off. Up till now I had been following our old tracks made in previous journeys, but the ground had become harder and it was difficult to distinguish them any longer. We were therefore obliged to steer by compass until such time as we should sight the Three Sisters. For three hours we roared onwards, occasionally slowing down to bump over a rough watercourse, but there was no sign of the Sisters. It seemed a long time since we had seen any sign of our old tracks; having missed them we were unable to rediscover them. I kept up a meaningless conversation with Sanderson so as to hide my uneasiness from myself, for twice I had altered my course, first to the right, then to the left, in the endeavour to pick up the track, but without success.

Suddenly my companion gripped my arm. 'Look!' he cried, 'What's that?' For a moment I could not spare a glance for what he was pointing to. 'We're making for something that's shining!' he said. Then I looked towards the distant point which he indicated. 'Good lord!' I gasped, 'it's the line! We're making straight for the line!' With a violent wrench I swung her to the left, and on we raced away madly. My companion stood up in his place and signalled frantically to the driver of 'Blue Mist' to follow us closely. Then we leapt the cars like hares away from those gleaming metals, regardless of what lay in our path.

However, we now had some idea of where we were, and with the aid of my compass I set my course in a direction which would bring us across the old track sooner or later. Presently we sighted the Three Sisters, and an hour before sunset we limped across the line below Maan. We still had to get to Aba el Lissan before dark, so without delaying for a moment we drove straight on, and just as the sun went down we were rewarded by the sight of the camp of our half-battery which had remained behind when the rest of us had gone to Azrak. Cries of delight echoed amongst the granite rocks as we drove in, for to these men, in their loneliness and ignorance of what was going on at the front, we were angels of light. Hardly had we pulled up when we were plied with eager questions: Had we brought orders for a move? Where had we come from? Where were we going? I handed the sealed orders to the officer in charge and he made prompt arrangements to have the gold loaded on my tender, together with some other supplies.

The next day at dawn we left again for the north.

Chapter Twenty-Six
The Raid On Deraa

As we came again in sight of Azrak and the troops massed there I was astonished at the extent of their camps. Egyptian Camel Corps and Gurkhas from India were mixed up with some French Moroccans and with swarms of the Arabs of the desert, in a seething horde of warriors. A car made its appearance, coming out to meet us, and as I watched its approach I cried suddenly, 'It's the Skipper in a Ford!'

With a squealing of brakes the two Rolls-Royces were brought to a standstill. Lawrence's car stopped too, and he got down and came towards us. When his glance fell on the boxes of gold which we had brought he murmured, 'Splendid!' and that word meant more to us than all the highfalutin rubbish handed out by verbose brass-hats on a parade which had been preceded perhaps by hours of button-polishing and general hysteria. He now explained to us that with our load he would buy the Sakhr tribe and their corn for the attack on Deraa.

Railway lines from Damascus, Maan and Haifa met at Deraa, and the raid which Lawrence had planned had as its chief object the cutting of all three of these a few days before the opening of Allenby's offensive on 19th September. The job of disabling the line south of Deraa was given to the Egyptian Camel Corps, the Gurkhas, and two armoured cars with tenders. Lawrence's plan was for the Gurkhas to rush a block-house under cover of darkness, and to hold it while the Egyptians destroyed as much of the line as they could before dawn. The armoured cars and tenders were to cover the attack, the latter carrying a large supply of gun-cotton. At dawn we were to retire to the eastward and rejoin Lawrence with the main army.

On 12th September we moved out from Azrak in the direction of Deraa, which lay sixty miles to the north west, and at nightfall we encamped behind a low range of hills. The armoured cars in their bivouac were surrounded by dark, turbaned Indians, who passed most of the hours of waiting in sharpening their murderous-looking knives, the only weapon they carried with them. Every now and then they ran a finger along the edge, and a horrible grin of satisfaction would spread on their evil-looking faces. Strange tales went round that they were in the habit of dipping the point of their knives in poison before going into action; that they never unsheathed their weapons without shedding blood, and so on. Somebody wanted to lay odds that no Turks would face this crowd, crawling in on them in the darkness, unseen except for their gleaming eyes and knives. The moment their war-cry was heard the Turks would flee shrieking into the night.

The raid had a tame ending, however, for a mob of Bedouins encamped on our line of advance refused to give us passage, and as it would have been impossible to carry on with the operation after a stand-up fight beforehand with another enemy, even had we been prepared for this, retirement was the only course left open to us. We met Lawrence with this bad news at dawn next day, just as he and the rest were setting out from Azrak themselves to raid the Deraa-Damascus line. He at once decided to see the job through himself, and chose two bridges near Umtaiye as the point for the demolition.

By 15th September the Arab army was on the march to envelop Deraa from the north, and just after noon on that day the two armoured cars and two tenders, which were to carry out the raid south of Deraa alone, moved to a ridge at Umtaiye, which overlooked the line. Here Lawrence got out of my tender, and taking a large quantity of gun-cotton, mounted into one of the armoured cars. The other armoured car was to cover his advance to the bridges by engaging the Turks in a block house which guarded the line at that point.

A deafening roar grew in the air as we were making these arrangements, and a squadron of British aeroplanes could be seen making north towards Deraa. This sight heartened us considerably, and away went the two armoured cars towards the line, leaving us in the tenders to watch them. They bucketed and plunged over the rough ground, growing smaller as they receded from us. Suddenly the driver of the other tender cried, 'Look! What's that?' I glanced in the direction of his pointing finger and saw a long caravan of camels at no great distance. I did not like the look of this, so after a moment's hesitation we ran to the top of the ridge and began to do our best to attract the attention of Lawrence by making signals. But no sign came to us that he had seen us, and the caravan was getting nearer and nearer every minute. I did not like the look of things, and I felt that the armoured cars should be warned at all costs, so I told the man in the other tender to get behind his machine gun and stay there, while I drove out in front to report to Lawrence. Without more ado I started off, rounded the bend of the hill, and with the heavy load swaying the car this way and that in a wild dance, drove straight in the track of the armoured cars.

The going was terribly bad; huge stones lay everywhere, and watercourses had to be negotiated continually, and as I drew nearer to the railway a hail of spent bullets whistled about me and fell in the dust. I drove right down to the bridge, and as soon as I had stopped Lawrence ran up and said, 'I hope you've got the gun-cotton.'

'Yes,' I cried, 'I've got it.' By this time I had completely forgotten in the excitement what I had really come here for, and also my lonely friend on the ridge. Backwards and forwards we ran, laden with gun-cotton, regardless of everything except the job in hand. 'This is a splendid bridge,' said Lawrence, as he jammed six blocks of gun-cotton into a drainage hole. I looked round, saw the armoured cars covering us, and agreed with him. 'I doubt whether they'll have the time or the inclination to repair it before Deraa falls,' he said confidently.

Suddenly there was a violent burst of machine-gun fire, but it was only the armoured cars firing at the Turks in a trench before the block-house. These, not knowing whether they were expected to run away or surrender, had got up in their trench, apparently to make inquiries. They tried again, more successfully, after a few minutes, and I saw them approaching the cars with their hands held up above their heads.

Half a dozen charges were fired under the arches, and the bridge was put out of action for a long time to come. 'That'll fix it!' said Lawrence, as we mounted into the tender again. The prisoners were packed aboard the cars and we drove away. I was doubtful of the ability of my car to carry the extra weight over the very rough ground; but we were nearly always overloaded in these days, and I drove on grimly, hoping for the best. I swung her first to one side, then to the other, so as to avoid the many watercourses which criss-crossed over the ground, while our prisoners hung on as best they could. All at once there was a violent crackling of breaking wood and rending of metal, and two of the prisoners were flung off with a heap of gear. The car had come to a standstill. Was this to be the end of the car which had carried me in all sorts of rough conditions for twenty thousand miles? Lawrence and I glanced at one another, and without a word got out. I made a quick inspection and found that she had broken a spring bracket. The case seemed hopeless. Lawrence meanwhile signalled to the armoured cars, which by this time were some distance ahead.

I stood looking at my disabled car and racking my brains to think of some plan to get her going again. At last I began feverishly flinging the load off her to right and left, while the men of the other cars, which had now come up, turned to and lent me a hand. Then I seized the hydraulic jack, which was always kept handy in the fore part of the cockpit, and placed it under the lowest corner of the chassis, at the same time calling for packing. Various kinds of objects were handed to me, and with the help of some of these I managed to get the required height. Lawrence, eager to help, seized the jack handle and began to lever it up and down. Slowly the car rose; more packing was placed underneath, and we repeated the operation until she stood nearly level.

We quickly removed the special detachable running board from the opposite side; its tapered end would make it easier to insert underneath the cantilever spring, and through to the opposite side.

We were streaming with sweat, but the chassis was still not quite high enough, though the jack was fully extended. We had no more packing, and I looked about frantically for some other means of raising it. I grabbed the running-board, pushed the wedge end just underneath the spring, and began to lever it gingerly, fearing lest it should break. 'Get ready to push the board in!' I cried, and they all got into position on the word. 'Now then! All together!' I gave the order, and as I levered her up they all pushed, and in went the board. I took a fresh purchase and levered again, and this time they forced it home to its limit; but about six feet of it still projected from the side. We had no saw, and it was Lawrence's turn now. He drew his revolver and fired bullets into the board in line until it could be snapped off easily. The result of our exertions was excellent: the car stood squarely as though it was uninjured, and I sprang into the driving seat, eager to test my handiwork. It stood the strain perfectly well, but when we camped at Umtaiye that night I seized the opportunity to make a stronger job of my repairs. I strengthened the running board with short lengths of my four-inch pole, wedging them tightly between the fixed running-board and the one carrying the weight. These we bound in place so firmly with telegraph wire that the car carried normal loads right up to the end of the campaign at Damascus. The line between Deraa and Amman had been cut without any cost except the explosives. Lawrence, wandering about my improvised workshop, scribbled in a tattered note-book and asked me questions about the car. He gave me all the credit for saving the car, but I replied that he, by giving me a free hand and refraining from issuing orders, had made it possible to save it, and I thanked him for his consideration. At this he burst into a hearty laugh, a delightful, friendly laugh. I thought, 'What a man!' He took men at their true value, and paid no heed to outward rank or social position, and it was this attitude that made him not only a friend and helper, but a great leader. He never asked anybody to do what they could not understand, and in all cases of extreme hazard he himself took the danger-post.

We now had to rejoin the Arab army at Arar, north of Deraa; and early on the following morning we set out over the roughest ground I had yet attempted. Sheer doggedness upheld the men, but I, for one, felt certain that soon the cars must give way under the terrible strain. My great wish was to see them in at the finish of the campaign, but the going in this place had become almost impossible. We limped over masses of jagged rock and crawled painfully along the bottom of rock strewn watercourses, my steering-wheel whirling this way and that continually, tearing my hands till the blood flowed from them. Lawrence sat huddled in the seat beside me, and as the car rose and fell with sickening thuds, jarring us so that our bones almost rattled, I knew well enough that he was another silent sufferer, although he had no responsibility for the car's safety. Occasionally he uttered a few words of encouragement which really were encouraging - not an easy thing for a passenger to do with success. The morning was still young when we caught up with the Arab army. They were on the point of attacking a redoubt guarding the railway, and we watched them from the top of a hill. They met with stiff opposition from the Turks, but this was soon overcome with the help of a few rounds from the guns of the French Moroccan Battery. In a few minutes the place was in the hands of the Arabs, and then everyone settled down to enjoy the feeling of victory. The line had to be thoroughly disabled, as it was the main line of communication of the Turkish army; but before more than one charge of explosive had been fired the Turks in Deraa, four miles away, sent a reconnaissance aeroplane over to see what we were up to. Very soon after this had taken back its report no less than eight other machines came over to bomb us. We scattered in all directions, and I hastily crawled underneath my tender. In the next few minutes a number of bombs crashed down, sending up columns of smoke and earth, but they did not appear to do much damage, and the nearest to me was fifty yards away. The Egyptians went on with their demolition of the line.

All at once a British machine appeared on the scene; it flew over the railway line to westward, and the Turkish machines followed it, leaving us and the Arabs to carry on with our plans. Presently, however, we saw our man flying back again, followed by three of the enemy, the rattle of whose machine guns could be plainly heard. Every one rushed to a flat piece of ground, the nearest we could come to, and began to clear the stones off it, and roll out the landing signal, so that the pilot might come down, as it appeared to be neck or nothing with him. He came down and appeared to land well, but went over in a somersault. We ran to help, expecting to find the pilot injured, but he got out of the machine himself, and was found to be unhurt except for a few cuts. He dismounted his guns and placed them in a Ford tender, together with the ammunition, and was driven away just in time to escape a bomb which one of the following Turks dropped on his damaged machine.

Chapter Twenty-Seven
Harrying Communications

Lawrence and most of the Arab army moved away to the west, with the object of destroying Muzerib station on the Haifa line, leaving our Battery in reserve on the hill at Arar. The Turkish aircraft bombed them continually as they went, but they kept steadily on their way, and after nightfall we saw the flashes of their exploding charges on the railway line.

In the morning a messenger arrived from Lawrence, requesting that the armoured cars be moved south again, to Umtaiye, whither he intended to work his way, thus completing the encirclement of Deraa. A tormenting day followed, for no car could survive long undamaged on that terrible going, which we had already crossed once in the opposite direction. One after another of them broke down, as some part or other gave way under the strain. First a shorn back axle brought a car to a standstill; then another was held up by the breaking of a steering drop arm, snapped like a match stick. More than once we had to set to work to make one sound car out of two which were disabled, by transferring sound parts from one to the other. The hopelessly disabled cars were left like spent camels in the desert after their loads and crews had been distributed amongst the others.

Lawrence duly met us at Umtaiye, and the strain and excitement of the last days was plainly written on his face, as it was on the faces of all of us. For three days and nights we had hardly slept at all, and our time had been spent in a continual hectic rushing from place to place, with hardly a moment's respite and with very little food. But with such an example as that given us by the Skipper, whose unflinching will carried him through greater physical hardships and mental strain than anything we had to endure, it was impossible for us to give in or let our minds play with thoughts of ease. His appearance among us always had the effect of immediately lightening our burdens, but no other relief was possible.

In the early morning following our arrival at Umtaiye I was lying half asleep on my improvised bed in the front seat of the tender when I was roused by a violent explosion close at hand. Raising myself on one elbow I looked towards the railway and saw a train moving on it. As I looked there was a flash and a puff of smoke, and another shell whistled towards us and burst a few yards from my tender. They had a gun on the train and were firing it at us as they moved down the line. I leapt from my bed like a rabbit, and we were soon all on the move. At first our motley crowd treated this attack as an ordinary incident in the day's work, but when an aeroplane got up and flew over to spot for the gunners on the train we began to increase our pace, and soon our easy gait had changed to a hustle. In a wild scramble of camels, men and cars we presently drew out of range, and the aeroplane disappeared.

Presently we drew together again and halted, but we had hardly begun to prepare our breakfast when Lawrence called for volunteers to investigate the Turkish aerodrome, where the spotting machine and two others had been seen to land. Leaving the tea and freshly opened tins of bully beef, every man offered to go, but there was a look on the faces of most which told plainly that they felt a bit sick at having to leave their breakfast when it was just getting ready. Lawrence doubtless read the subtle anguish in the eyes of all the eager volunteers, and their trouble was relieved when a grin spread over his face, and after a pause, to get the full taste of the situation, he said, 'Of course, I meant after breakfast.'

When the hasty meal had been eaten, the two cars which

had been selected moved cautiously towards the railway line, with closed cut-outs, until they came within rifle range. Looking through the driving slits the men in them could see three aeroplanes on the landing ground beyond. But our cars had been seen, and almost at once two of the machines rose in the air and flew away, untouched by the fire of the machine gunners. The third aeroplane could not be started quickly enough to get away, and as our men loosed belt after belt of ammunition at them the pilot and observer left it and took cover under the railway embankment. The machine was riddled with our bullets.

Soon afterwards the other two machines returned from Deraa with a load of bombs, which they rained down on the armoured cars; and when at last the latter came limping back with damaged tyres and paint to where we waited, we gave them a rousing cheer.

We were bombed incessantly after this at our camp near Umtaiye, but we had to remain there so as to keep the railway junction of Deraa in a state of disablement. The place was haunted by us, as by flitting ghosts. Every now and then we visited the scene of our various demolitions on the line and presented the Turkish repair gangs with a belt or two of ammunition to check their activities. But our position was precarious, and a really powerful air attack might well scatter us for good and all, camped as we were in the open desert, with no cover of any sort.

Another danger was the dilapidated condition of our cars, and I took an opportunity of speaking earnestly to Lawrence about this. Only three of our Rolls-Royces were running now, and these were patched with parts of the others which lay derelict miles away in the desert. The abandoned cars had probably already been made permanently useless by the mischievous Arabs, but those which we still had in use might be kept going. If they were to be in at the finish of the campaign, however, we must have the necessary materials for repairing them without delay. I put this before Lawrence as forcibly as I could, and he answered quietly, 'Yes; I have seen your difficulties. If you will make out a detailed indent I'll see what can be done.' I duly handed him the list. It consisted of almost enough spares to make several complete chassis, and included such items as back axles, steering gears, drop arms, magnetos, and a multitude of others.

On the afternoon of 18th September we started off for Umm Surab, intent on destroying another stretch of the line. Lawrence sat beside me and pointed out the way. He seemed unusually silent, and suddenly, for the first time in my experience of him, he showed signs of being at a loss. He had lost the way, and all his efforts to find it, whether to the right, to the left, or straight on, were of no avail. We had come into a complicated maze of small valleys, and could find neither the railway nor our own troops, who were to assist in the demolition. At last, when night was falling, we saw a light, and making towards it we found at last that it came from Mafrak station, some distance south of our objective. From here we moved northward again, following a train which came out of the station.

As soon as it was quite dark flashes and the noise of explosions on the line revealed to us the position of our troops. Presently the train was seen coming back, and the armoured cars opened fire on it, but with little effect. One of the cars had its petrol tank pierced by a bullet, and some time was taken up in plugging it before we could proceed.

On the following morning Lawrence left for Azrak in one of the armoured cars for the purpose of meeting an aeroplane which would take him to Palestine for a conference with Allenby, whose great offensive had now opened. The armoured cars were left to await his return at Umm Surab, and for some hours all was quiet on our front, and we were able to sleep.

Very early the next morning we were awakened by a scuffling of excited Arabs, and suddenly somebody shouted, 'Aeroplanes up!' I scrambled up to see what all the commotion was about, and saw an ordinary aeroplane and a flying monster, apparently coming down to land. The Arabs scattered in all directions, but somebody cried out, 'It's a British machine! It's dropping landing signals!' We dashed forward to roll out the T sign and clear the largest stones off a flat space of ground; and the great Handley Page aircraft came lower still, until it seemed to fill the sky with its wide-spreading wings. We watched in astonishment while she sank slowly, and at last she took the ground with hardly a bump. We ran to lend a hand, and I saw Lawrence peering over the side of the small aeroplane's fuselage, for the second machine had now landed beside the giant.

The skipper brought astonishing news: Allenby had already taken Nablus, Beisan, Afule, Semakh and Haifa. This information spread like wildfire, and the Rualla and the rest of the Arabs became madly excited and demanded to be allowed to advance on Damascus without further delay. I wondered whether we should ever get our cars to Damascus. At the first opportunity I got close to Lawrence and gave a pull at his cloak. He looked round and smiled when he saw me. 'Got the stuff?' I said, staring at him earnestly. He smiled on me in silence for another moment or two, and then said, 'It should be inside the Handley Page.' I dashed up to the half-open door of the great aeroplane and took a look inside the fuselage. The huge cavern seemed half full of cases of heavy spare parts. I had never supposed that such weights could be carried through the air, and I was astounded. Everything I wanted was there, and forty cases of petrol as well. And Lawrence was standing at my elbow, calmly asking if that would do. I said, 'With all that we can salvage every car,' and eventually we did so.

The great mass of warriors of the Rualla tribe now moved

up to the line from their camp at Azrak, and while they advanced across it to the north of Deraa, we in the armoured cars moved again to the south, where we indulged in yet another wild orgy of railway destruction. We screamed like demons as the air was rent with the roar of our explosions, and bits and pieces flew in all directions. One of the bridges had been almost completely repaired by means of wooden trestles, but a fierce volley from the armoured cars scattered the repair gang, and we drove to the scene of their useless labours, and set fire to their handiwork.

After this the Turks seemed to give up all thought of putting the line in working order again, but we continued to use loads of gun-cotton on it, scouring along the line in a continual mad hustle. A block-house south of Mafrak was found to be still held by the enemy, so Lawrence drove down that way in a car to clean it up, getting bombed with hand grenades in the process. And just as we continued to batter the railway, so the Turks continued to bomb the desert at Umtaiye, although the bulk of our army had gone over the line to westward. In the night a heavy droning in the air told that the Handley Page was up and doing, and soon many sharp flashes and dull, hollow booms in the direction of Mafrak gave us the news that she was bombing the station there.

Rumour reached us that the main body of the Turkish Fourth Army was evacuating Amman in disorder and retreating northward, harassed by the Arabs. The armoured cars were ordered back to Azrak to await there the fall of Deraa, but the two Rolls-Royce tenders were to remain at the disposal of Lawrence and the other leaders. Few of the cars reached Azrak, however, for they ran into a mob of Turkish cavalry on the way, and after rounding them up they were obliged to march them to the railway to find food for them. A few escaped and managed to reach Deraa.

The Turks were by this time completely broken, and our

feverish hustle to Damascus had begun.

Chapter Twenty-Eight
The Race To Damascus

Under Allenby's hammering most of the survivors of the Turkish army had retreated through Deraa, hoping, no doubt, that railway communication to Damascus would still be available by the time they got there. Lawrence's army had destroyed the railway, however, and the exhausted enemy hastened as fast as they could to get clear of the place again on their feet. The clothes of most of them were in rags, and they were starving, and fainting for lack of sleep; and when the wild Arab wave broke on them they could do almost nothing to protect themselves. They could not even halt and make a proper effort to beat off the attacks, for close behind them the British Desert Mounted Corps pressed steadily forward to annihilate them.

Throughout 27th September we hung about on the slopes to the north of Deraa, waiting for our call, and as night closed down strange, hollow noises disturbed the quiet in the direction of the town, and flaming lights glowed there. The distant thunders of guns could be occasionally heard, and the air was filled with an uncanny strangeness. Nobody grumbled about having to do night guard, and, in fact, most of us were awake all night. We could hear muffled explosions, and occasionally sharp tongues of flame leapt skyward. There were sharp, cracking noises, like the breaking of twigs. We were fascinated by Deraa and could not take our eyes off it. Most of our Arabs had swept away in that direction at sunset, and Lawrence, too, after making a brief appearance among us, had gone off again on his camel.

Dawn came, and we found ourselves still on the hills, uncertain of what was happening in front of us or behind, and hardly knowing what we ought to do. We supposed that Deraa was in the hands of the Arabs, but we ourselves felt lost, as though we had been left high and dry on an uninhabited island by an ebbing tide. Then we saw men hastening from all directions towards the town, and full realisation seemed to come to us. There was a feverish rush to start the engines, and in a few moments we were picking our way gingerly in single file down the treacherous slope to the walled enclosures below. On coming close to those we found ourselves running on a properly metalled road for the first time in many months. We made the best of our way towards the aerodrome, where we hoped to acquire some petrol; and when we reached it we found that it was infested with the cream of the Arab army, who staggered here and there under the weight of their loot, their eyes glaring with the lust of plunder. Near one of the hangars a fight was in progress concerning the ownership of parts torn from the wreck of a crashed machine.

A similar argument was going on round a fifty-gallon barrel. 'Come on!' I shouted, 'that looks like petrol.' As usual, our approach was viewed with sullen scowls by the Arabs, and as they had found the barrel first we decided it would be more diplomatic to let them find out what it contained. They could hardly have a use for it themselves. We waited and watched while the mob hammered and wrenched at the bung. But they were unable to make much impression on it, and eventually most of them gave up in disgust, thinking, no doubt, that their energies might be used more profitably elsewhere. A few, however, struggled on doggedly in the attempt to open the barrel. At last one of the cleverer members of the Battery stood up and waved a tin of bully beef in the air, at the same time shouting to the Arabs and making signs to them that he was prepared to exchange his tin of meat for their barrel. The effect was excellent, for one of the Arabs ran up and received the tin, and immediately all the rest fell upon him and tried to wrest it from him. This was our opportunity, and we closed on the barrel without further delay. However, it was only half full of very inferior petrol.

Parts of Deraa were in flames still, and the whole place seemed to be in ruins. Dead animals lay everywhere, most of them hacked as though the Turks had used them for food, and hardly a single building remained undamaged after the place had been half the previous night in the hands of our Arabs. We inspected the engine workshops and railway sidings with interest, but even there everything was in the greatest disorder.

In Deraa we waited for orders, which showed no sign of coming, until at last our acting commander decided that we should move northward as an escort for Feisal in his green Vauxhall. The Arab prince had now arrived from Azrak, and the job of acting as his escort seemed such a civilized one, after what we had been accustomed to, that we were all delighted with the prospect. Moreover, it seemed to us that we were to accompany a king in triumph to his throne. We were a ragamuffin crew for such an occasion though, and my car had a dangerous list to one side. Pieces of telegraph wire and frayed rope ends, with which she was tied together, dangled from her as she moved.

We drove out and took our way to the north, and before nightfall the signs of the beaten Turks and their pursuers were to be seen in all directions. Stragglers from the enemy's rearguard, some dying, others already dead, were met continually, and numbers sat or lay by the wayside, utterly spent.

We halted at last on the dusty track, which had been churned up by the hooves and wheels of both armies, and tried to sleep among the dead and dying. I doubt whether any of us closed our eyes. I did not sleep a wink, and never was dawn more welcome to me than that which at long last followed this grim night. With scarcely a glance to right or left we started up the cars and hurried on our way through the horrifying sights everywhere presented, postponing even the morning cup of tea until we should reach less sickening surroundings. Half-naked, festering bodies lay in all directions, some with staring eyes and discoloured with blood.

Our new job of acting as bodyguard to Feisal kept us from joining in the actual pursuit of the enemy; and the Arabs, increasing by thousands almost hourly, had carried it on swiftly by themselves. At times we came in sight of batches of Turkish prisoners, but the Arabs had driven the rearguard far to the north. We saw nothing of Lawrence, but occasionally an Arab rode up to report to Feisal that all was going well in the pursuit.

We had left the arid desert and were now traversing the fertile plains of Hauran. Only to the east the bare mountain slopes reminded us that the desert was not far away.

Near sunset we came under a mountain ridge, and here we halted and made our camp. Most of us were in high spirits, and excitement became intense when somebody came along and gave us the wonderful news that Bulgaria had been knocked right out of the war.

In the morning we skirted the ridge, moving at an easy pace and making occasional halts. The road here was strewn with broken-down transport wagons and derelict German cars, showing the helter-skelter nature of the enemy's retreat. An Arab brought the story that Damascus had already been set on fire by the Turks and was burning fiercely. We increased our pace at this news, for there was nothing which we would not have believed of the enemy.

Presently we saw more horsemen coming towards us, and as we closed on them they gave us the news that Damascus was in the hands of the Arabs; and a little further on we came in sight of the city itself. Its buildings shone white in the sunlight, and all around it lay a great expanse of dark green orchards. Feisal sat calmly in his green car, his dignified features showing no trace of any feeling at the great news, and I thought that he was a fit man to mount a throne. Already he looked a king. The Arabs, mounted on horses, surrounded his car closely, and again the order was given to advance. Damascus was not burning, but was waiting to receive us. We moved away down the dusty road, the horsemen racing one another, or galloping in wide circles round the green Vauxhall and its escorting cars. Soon we came to the first of the cultivated fields, and at last entered the southern, or Meidan, quarter of the city.

Lawrence had already been two days in Damascus, having entered it while we were still at Deraa, waiting for orders; and he and Allenby, and a score of other generals, had received an hysterical welcome from the people. But the enthusiasm was not all drained away for when we brought the Arab prince in, the groups of men whom we passed stared at us amazed, and then seemed to go raving mad. They threw their tarbooshes into the air, waved their arms, danced a hornpipe, and shouted and screamed at the top of their voices. As we came to the centre of the city the crowd grew so thick that the leading car could hardly force a way, and in the open square by the Town Hall the roaring and screaming of the citizens was deafening. I saw a cart being forced through the thick of the mob and out of the back of it hung four or five pairs of human legs, stiff and lifeless. By steady pressure we forced a way through the square, and came to the Town Hall. Here Feisal got out of his car, and as he mounted the steps of the building there fell a slight hush, and then a roar, which seemed to shake the whole city, burst forth from the straining crowd. Several people forced their way through to us and followed the prince; and when they had spoken to him he descended the steps again and seated himself in his car. We then drove further, as directed by a guide, and came to the chief hotel, where Allenby was waiting for his first meeting with Feisal. When he had gone inside, the crowd thinned a little, and we were able to drive along the bank of the river and cross a bridge, coming back by that way to the square. Here we saw, across the stream from the Town Hall, a building marked 'Hotel Jericho.' We got out to inspect it, and somebody said, 'Will it do, lads?' There was no reply in words, but so far as I was concerned I gained the second floor in less than half a dozen seconds, in time to bag a beautiful bed with a spring mattress in a large, airy room with a clean tiled floor. The others secured similar accommodation for themselves, except a few of the slowest, who had mattresses on the floor.

The ground floor of the building consisted of a row of empty shops or stables, which were just large enough to hold an armoured car each; so we backed all our vehicles into them like fire-engines, so that they would be ready to be driven out at a moment's notice. From my upper window I could see my old friend Nuri, and also Jaafar, Auda, and the rest going in and out of the Town Hall. Not long afterwards we saw Feisal there, standing at the top of the steps with Lawrence, while the mob howled around them.

Then a man came along peddling cooked beetroots, and I lusted after them, but had no money. 'Try him with bully,' said somebody. I found a tin of meat in my car and offered it to the pedlar, and as soon as he saw it his eyes lit up with joy, and he gave me the best beetroot on his tray in exchange for it.

The same night Lawrence looked in to say farewell to us all, for he was leaving the city in the morning. 'Good-bye,' he said, as he gripped my hand warmly. 'My job here's done. I shall not be wanted any more. Well, we've had great fun together, haven't we?' I mumbled a reply, and as he went away our situation seemed to be drained suddenly of every drop of interest.

During the following days Damascus remained in a ferment of excitement, and there was scuffling all over the place. The Arabs fired off their rifles every now and then as an amusement, and the whole population seemed to spend most of its time in the streets. To add to the excitement one of my comrades amused himself now and then by throwing bullets extracted from rifle cartridges through the upper windows of the Town Hall, by means of a catapult. It was certainly funny to watch an official inside pick up a bullet, which perhaps had actually struck him, and pass it excitedly round to his friends for their inspection. The view taken by them appeared to be that somebody was trying to murder them all with a rifle fitted with a silencer. But eventually they must have noticed that the bullets were not marked by rifling, and one day three officers of the Arab police paid us a call, bringing one of the bullets with them. They stamped up our stairs and demanded to see the officer in charge. I said that perhaps I would do, as I held the exalted rank of lance-corporal. At this they spat on our floor and demanded to be supplied with an officer of high rank. They must have found one in the end, though it was not with our assistance, for a court of inquiry was held - but the culprit was never discovered.

Chapter Twenty-Nine
Peace

All through October and most of November we remained in Damascus, and almost nightly we were called out to assist in quelling disturbances in the city. I was tired to death of the empty, meaningless army life and longed for freedom again. Lawrence had long since gone, and with him went the only influence that made my existence as a soldier at all bearable. And the other men in the Battery were never tired of talking about him, and regretting that he was no longer among us. I spoke to the commanding officer with a view to getting myself demobilized, but time went on and nothing happened; and then one day the Battery received orders to entrain for Palestine. It was a novel experience to find ourselves travelling on the line we had so often blown up, and probably on the trucks at which we had fired our guns. We looked out eagerly for the places we knew - Arar, Deraa, Muzerib - and noted the repairs which had been carried out in each one of them.

As we passed over the Yarmuk bridge I peered down into the deep ravine below and up at the steep slope of the left bank, and thought of Lawrence crawling down the latter in the dead of night, while the Turkish sentry paced in blissful ignorance beside the track.

We came to the southern end of the Sea of Galilee, and here the train stopped for a long time, so that we were able to bathe in a warm spring. We were in the middle of this when the engine whistle screamed shrilly, and we had to get into our clothes as fast as we could and return to the train. There we learnt that a telegram had just been received from Damascus, recalling the whole Battery immediately, and that the train was to return as it stood, as soon as the engine had been changed to the other end. In this disappointment my commanding officer came to my rescue nobly. He knew that I wanted very much to get away, and now, coming close to me, he told me to remain behind, where I was, and get on the first train which passed down the line to Ramleh. He would send a special order for my demobilization, and I could then proceed to Port Said, and so home to England.

I hurriedly took my belongings out of my car, shook hands with my friends, jumped off the train; and then watched it disappear round a bend in the steep track – bound once more for Damascus.

ALSO FROM LEONAUR
AVAILABLE IN SOFTCOVER OR HARDCOVER WITH DUST JACKET

RGW2 RECOLLECTIONS OF THE GREAT WAR 1914-18
WITH THE IMPERIAL CAMEL CORPS IN THE GREAT WAR
by Geoffrey Inchbald

The Story of a Serving Officer with the British 2nd Battalion Against the Senussi and During the Palestine Campaign.

SOFTCOVER : **ISBN** **1-84677-007-6**
HARDCOVER : **ISBN** **1-84677-012-2**

MCI THE MILITARY COMMANDER SERIES
JOURNALS OF ROBERT ROGERS OF THE RANGERS
by Robert Rogers

The Exploits of Rogers & the Rangers in his Own Words During 1755-1761 in the French & Indian War.

SOFTCOVER : **ISBN** **1-84677-002-5**
HARDCOVER : **ISBN** **1-84677-010-6**

EW3 EYEWITNESS TO WAR SERIES
THE KHAKEE RESSALAH
by Robert Henry Wallace Dunlop

Service & Adventure with the Meerut Volunteer Horse During the Indian Mutiny 1857-1858.

SOFTCOVER : **ISBN** **1-84677-009-2**
HARDCOVER : **ISBN** **1-84677-017-3**

WFI THE WARFARE FICTION SERIES
NAPOLEONIC WAR STORIES
by Sir Arthur Quiller-Couch

Tales of Soldiers, Spies, Battles & Sieges from the Peninsula & Waterloo Campaigns.

SOFTCOVER : **ISBN** **1-84677-003-3**
HARDCOVER : **ISBN** **1-84677-014-9**

AVAILABLE ONLINE AT
www.leonaur.com
AND OTHER GOOD BOOK STORES

Printed in the United Kingdom
by Lightning Source UK Ltd.
125902UK00001B/181/A